CONTENTS

Page

NOTE: the page references throughout are to *Winding Quest* unless they are preceded by the letters *'NW'* (*New World*).

The Bible in the Classroom

A Handbook to WINDING QUEST and NEW WORLD

Alan T. Dale

Oxford University Press 1972

Oxford University Press, Ely House, London W. 1

GLASGOW NEW YORK TORONTO MELBOURNE WELLINGTON
CAPE TOWN IBADAN NAIROBI DAR ES SALAAM LUSAKA ADDIS ABABA
DELHI BOMBAY CALCUTTA MADRAS KARACHI LAHORE DACCA
KUALA LUMPUR SINGAPORE HONG KONG TOKYO

Printed in Great Britain at
Fletcher and Son Ltd., Norwich

INTRODUCTION

This is a personal statement—it could hardly be otherwise. Although the making of *New World* began with the demand of students to have the gospel material they were dealing with in the classroom put into simple English so that the less verbally able children could read it easily, it was soon clear that there were other important matters to be dealt with.

Reading itself is much more than being able to recognize words; the words must really mean something to the reader. The dimension of the act of reading 'includes even more than gaining the meaning from the word . . . It includes perception, understanding, reaction and integration. By reaction and integration (is meant) that, once the reader has been stimulated by the author's words, he in turn vests the printed words with his own meaning by thinking about, judging, and critically evaluating the ideas he has read. So, reading is a complex process. A child reads not only with his eyes and voice, but with his experience and cultural heritage.' [1]

I quote an authoritative book on reading, because this was just what became clear. The passages from the New Testament I was translating for the students to use had been written two thousand years ago in a culture that has vanished; if their pupils were to learn anything from what they were reading, something more than just translating the words with a controlled vocabulary was needed.

But there was a further problem. The students themselves seemed to have a block between what we discussed together in college and what they attempted in the classroom. They might be revolutionary in college; they were traditional in the classroom. I began to realize that this was not due to any necessary unwillingness but to the lack of a tool. It was impossible, without great confusion and without raising all the wrong questions, to take even the gospel story and deal with it in the full translations (sometimes still the Authorized Version) available in the classrooms.

And then the whole question 'Why the Bible at all?' arose. And when you come to think of it (as students said)—why the Bible?

I can understand people who greet with amazement the suggestion

[1] Derek Thackray, *Readiness for Reading*, p.31.

that, if we want to find our feet in our twentieth-century debate about whether religion is really important and (if it is) what the word means, we might do much worse than turn to literature written two thousand or more years ago. In a world dominated by scientists, where the latest experiment and discussion crowns and outdates the research and discoveries of previous centuries, it seems strange to appeal, in any really helpful way, to records of what was thought and said and discovered so long ago. It is this feeling, I believe, which accounts for the decline in the habit of Bible reading among Christians themselves, and for the bewilderment of teachers trying to deal with it in the classroom. What can be the point of bothering with the army-lists of David's commandos, with trivial border fighting not even Egyptian or Assyrian records made any mention of, or with accounts of the creation of the world that had lost their significance millennia ago? Doesn't even Jesus sound remote and ineffectual in the massively changed and changing world of the twentieth century? And what can Paul have to say to us anyhow?

So it was not only a matter of language and comprehension—as if that was all that had to be dealt with; for students and young people alike, it was a matter of reading and understanding the Bible as a book worth reading and understanding today.

So the first tentative sketches that became *New World* were made— the account of Jesus in *Mark* and the sayings of Jesus which were the parts of the Bible the students were called upon to deal with most often.

I turned to my own experience. It was the work of scholars that had made it possible for me to take the Bible seriously at all. I can remember the time when, apart from a memorable story or an unforgettable line of poetry, the Bible seemed to me an outrageous book. I had no clue how to deal with its 'outrageousness', because I had been brought up in a strongly evangelical home where scholars of our own denominational tradition (Dr. A.S. Peake, for example, at whose feet I was later to sit) were suspect—and more than suspect. But it was just this work of scholars that made the Bible not only a living but a significant book to me. If this, I thought, was the way I myself had come, and if students, many of whom still came to college with little idea of biblical research, had found this same work liberating and illuminating too, then I must base my version of *Mark* and of the sayings of Jesus, for use by my students in secondary modern schools, on such research too, however simply it would have to be done. I turned to my marked Bible and to Dr. T.W. Manson.

And so the work which was to lead on (little as I knew it then) to *New World* and *Winding Quest* began, more than fifteen years ago.

If I am to give any worthwhile account of what I have tried to do to help young people and their teachers in these two books, I must deal with the whole argument that lies behind them. We must first be clear what kind of book the Bible is and what its function for religious life today is. What the Bible means to me explains why I determined, when the issues became clear to me, to be bold in the selection of biblical material and the arrangement of it. So I must first talk about the Bible—how I see it and how I read it, owing my understanding, as I do, to the help which the biblical scholars of this century have given me. I will then go on to show how I have tried to embody these insights in *New World* and *Winding Quest*; and finally show how I think these versions of the New and Old Testaments can be used in school.

But, before I do so, I ought to note the questions that have been raised about the very place of the Bible in religious education in the state schools and indicate where I stand. I should not be writing this book if I were not convinced that it has still not only an important but a central place in such education. But the impression is abroad that it has only a peripheral place there, and that its function is merely to illustrate the urgent themes that really occupy the centre of the debate that should go on in the classroom.

Recent research has shown, many would say, that the Bible presents so many difficulties that to deal with it effectively under school conditions is impossible. There is no gainsaying these difficulties, and there is no need here to do more than refer to Ronald Goldman's now famous *Religious Thinking from Childhood to Adolescence*, to the chapters 'Forgotten Knowledge' and 'Understanding Bible Doctrine' in Harold Loukes's *New Ground in Education*, and to the chapter 'The Bible in Religious Education' in Edwin Cox's *Changing Aims in Religious Education*. We must learn from this research.

There has also developed a feeling, in religious circles, that the Bible can only be understood within the religious community to which it belongs and in the vivifying atmosphere of worship; and that it is not

only misleading but improper to try to deal with it in any significant
way outside such an atmosphere. There is an important truth here that
I hope to deal with at another time; but there is also, it seems to me, a
grave misjudgment.

I believe that the Bible has a real place in the curriculum of the
school, not only in specific religious education but also in the newer
humanities courses (known by various names) that are such a hopeful
feature of the new school planning. I have no doubt for two reasons.

I believe that the Bible is not a private document but one of the great
public documents of the world. It is not the private possession of any
community. Most of it was spoken out on the public streets and open
to the world; what it records was not done 'in a corner'. I find it significant that serious readers who are not church members have seen some
of its truth more clearly than those who are; and as I read the history of
religious communities I am not impressed by their objectivity in their
Bible studies. I think that the Bible is most truly to be understood 'in
the open air of the world'. Its news is public news and its truth is
public truth.

Secondly, if I am to judge from my own experience—for myself and
for young people I have taught—I know no better introduction, if it is
properly read, to understanding how to think and live religiously. And
this, more than anything else, makes me convinced that it has a genuine
place in religious education which has been rightly defined as 'to help
pupils have a religious view of life and to make up their own minds on
religious questions'. With this I agree, though I would perhaps word it
differently. 'The aim of religious education would seem to be,' Edwin
Cox goes on, 'to help children to see, towards the end of their school
life, when they are able to think sufficiently deeply, that these are the
sort of questions that serious men have at times to ask; and also to give
them the information on which the answers may be based and to encourage them sincerely to make up their own minds for themselves.' [1]

It is, indeed, the situation in which we are now living and the questions that are now being debated and the decisions that now have to be
made which undoubtedly must be the heart of religious education today;

[1] Edwin Cox, *Changing Aims in Religious Education*, pp.66f.

we are not trying to imitate a vanished past but to be ourselves in our own present, facing our own religious questions and deepening our own insights and convictions. But how do we deal with religious questions? How do we learn to think and live religiously?

In the Bible, we can survey what I have called the first great debate about these very questions, and see it on the scale of a small world with all the living story out of which it emerged. Here we can see our human predicament, as it were, in miniature—the good that beckons us and the evil that threatens. Here we can see religious convictions in the making—the insights by which men can live and by which they can survive immense human disaster. Here we can see what is at stake, how men 'make sense of their story', what they mean by 'being aware of the presence of God'. The Bible is still, I believe, the best introduction to what is at stake. The reader who really knows how to read it is a religiously educated person.

But it is more. Here, in the Bible, are insights that have sustained men and women ever since they were first seen—and which sustain them still in our very different world. They are worth serious examination in twentieth-century schools.

CHAPTER ONE

THE WEALTH OF THE BIBLE

Approaching its importance

I had been brought up to think of the Bible as a 'holy' book—it was, in the circles where I moved 'The Holy Bible' as Palestine was always 'The Holy Land'. I can remember struggling with sayings from this 'holy' book which I read as though it was one book, written by one author, saying one thing from beginning to end. (Put crudely like this, few people would think this approach proper; yet the way we read it in church or as devotional reading has presuppositions not unlike those of the approach which I was taught.) Difficulties were got over by elaborate symbolism. I can remember my father, who was by no means extreme in his conservative views and for whom 'evolution' was not a bad word as it was for some of our friends, patiently explaining to me the correspondence between the 'days' of the first chapter of *Genesis* and the epochs of geological time.

What the scholars did for me was to show me what a human book it really was, and to set me free to let the Bible make its own impact on me. If I came to believe it a decisive and important book—a book to help me to find my way in my religious pilgrimage as a twentieth century man looking at my own world and beyond, sharing in its insights and achievements, its art and culture, and facing its immense disasters (two world wars and Belsen and the death of more than ten million people by violence of one sort or another in my lifetime)—this was my starting point. I had to go on to discover, the hard way, that there are stages in the reading and understanding of the Bible—and that there are no short cuts. We must not try to force meaning on the Bible.

I agree with David Jenkins (for this was the great lesson I learned):

> We ought to have understood that the Bible has no use so long as it is just treated as 'The Holy Bible'. We have to go beyond that and teach people to concentrate on it; not listen to it as if it was a 'holy book', but just listen to it. [1]

When I began to listen to it, I found it was a real book about real

---

[1] *Living with Questions*, p.188.

people, who could be placed in a real world at a real moment of time. I suppose that, before this, the world of the Bible had been, for me, a world in some way outside history—at least outside the history I found so fascinating in the history books in my father's library. Yet strangely enough, this discovery that the Bible was a very human book was an immense liberation. At least it was no fairytale.

But this very discovery, which was so liberating for me, is, in these more sophisticated days, a real obstacle. 'It's not a fairytale—all right. So what?'

Well, let us look at the Bible through the eyes of a modern theologian. The Bible

is the product of at least twelve hundred years of history, containing laws, narratives, romances, lyric poetry, proverbial wisdom, metaphysical speculation, moral instruction, prayers, liturgies, cosmogonies, family trees, sermons, predictions and heaven knows what else, written in three different languages . . . We cannot even say with certainty that all the writers were Jews or directly connected at some time in their lives with Judaism; and if they were, they undoubtedly borrowed from other faiths, cultures and philosophies. One book, indeed, has only the faintest link with the idea of God. And the whole of this literature stands, at its nearest, almost two thousand years away from us, and on the far side of several radical revolutions in human thought. [1]

Then where are we?

As I look back, I can see now that, mixed up as I was and long though it was before I really began to find my way (for years the Old Testament really meant little to me), I now realise that I slowly learned to approach it in stages; and in a real sense it is through these stages I approach it and read it still.

I read it as literature, literature that could hold its own with any literature from the ancient world and that could still haunt even unbelieving poets and artists.

I read it as the record of great insights. I can still remember the thrill of listening to Dr. Peake talk about Jeremiah and quoting

> desperate tides of a whole world's anguish
> forced through the channels of a single heart.

I read it (much later on) as the record of a great debate about

---

[1] John Austin Baker, *The Foolishness of God*, p.361

religion and what you mean when you use the word 'God', and of the discovery of the 'clue' in the witness of Jesus.

I read it as the foundation documents of the Christian community to which I belonged—this is what I am committed to, this is the work which began so long ago and which I must help to carry on.

Finally and at greatest depth, I read it as 'my history'.

Let me, then, first look at these stages and in the order in which I have just given them.

As literature

There is no short cut to the reading of great literature with critical awareness (that is, as something worth reading for its own sake). The Bible, whatever we think of it, contains important literature, and we must begin with it as such.

All literature from an age or from a tradition other than our own needs to be read in the light of what those who have studied that tradition or age have to tell us about it.

The Bible comes to us as a selection from the literature of a small highland people who survived (as the Greeks did) the disasters of history and defied the stupidities and brutalities of great military empires. Their voice still speaks across the centuries, although the shouts of the soldiers who burned their villages have long been silent and the cities they feared long lain in ruins. No literature is just 'literature'; it is the voice of men and women. The Bible is 'protest' literature.

If we are to listen to them, we must take note of the manner of their speech. It is here that scholars come to our aid. They have not only set before us, in most vivid and unexpected detail, the world out of which the Bible emerged, but they have shown us how varied were the literary forms poet and historian, priest and prophet, writer and editors used. It is surprising to realize how recent much of this knowledge is. We have become aware of the nature of Hebrew poetry only in the last hundred years (though it was actually rediscovered in the eighteenth century), and it is only since 1923 that we have begun to grasp that Jesus himself was a poet.

This is important. To know whether, for example, what you are reading is poetry or prose makes (or should make) all the difference to

the way in which you read it or, as a teacher, deal with it in the classroom. And so with all the other types of literary form—legend and myth,
tribal tradition and tribal poetry, popular story or contemporary narrative, historical survey or editorial comment, parable or poem, visionary
writing or diary or letter. The Bible is not a compendium of 'eternal
truths' but the voices of men and women speaking from their hearts. It
is the record of a search for the meaning of human tragedy (the death of
two cities in the Old Testament, and the death of a young man one
Friday afternoon in an occupied country in the New Testament); and
right or wrong, it is worth reading for its own sake.

As a record of important insights

Secondly, here is the record of some of the profoundest insights into
the meaning of human existence that have come down to us from the
past. We turn to Greece to listen to men whose insights lie behind the
world we have inherited; we turn to Palestine to listen to men who have
had no less an influence in the making of our world. To read and discuss
(as scholars have made it possible for us to do) what men like Amos and
Isaiah and Jeremiah had to say; to sit again at the feet of Jesus as we see
him through the memories and reports of his friends—this should be
part of any course of liberal studies. Here are no academics lecturing to
bright students but men of profound insight talking with common
people in street and house. They have been hidden between the covers
of a 'holy book'; they still need to be set free to speak directly to
young people and ordinary readers.

It is sometimes suggested that if we approach the Bible in this way,
which is simply the way in which we would approach any important
records of human experience, we bring its 'authority' into disrepute or
into question. The very opposite is the truth. It is only in this way that
any 'authority' the Bible has for men and women today can become
clear and unmistakable to them. It must speak to their conscience.

As debate and clue

The Bible comes to us in two parts—the Old Testament and the New
Testament. Both are part of one story—for Jesus himself died as a Jew
and the early Christian communities began as sectarian groups of the
wider first-century Jewish community. Yet each exists in its own right:

the Old Testament is the religious literature of the Hebrew and Jewish people; the New Testament is the legacy of the scattered Christian communities (for whom also the Old Testament was 'scripture') when they had established their independence and were determining where they stood.

Yet both these separate collections, with their obvious and real differences, have profound links with one another. It was because of these links that Christians kept both Testaments as their authoritative scripture, the Old Testament for them foreshadowing the New. [1] Let us put the relationship in this way.

The Old Testament is the record of the first great debate about the meaning of human existence. It springs, as we have said, from the tragic story of a small highland people; the event without which there would have been no Old Testament at all, was the death of their capital city, Jerusalem, in 586 B.C.E., and the extinction of their political independence. In a sense, their records are a recapitulation of the human predicament; and the question which they raise is the age-old question of the worthwhileness of human experience, the world being the sort of world it actually is. We owe it to the Israelite people and their outstanding minds that this question was set in so unforgettable a form. Here for the first time we listen to a debate about what you mean when you use the world 'God', what 'religion' is about, whether there is good religion and bad religion and how you tell the difference between the two, what is the place of man in the world and whether history has any enduring meaning.

The important thing is that the Israelites got the question right— answers are no good unless you really know what the question is. [2] Here in this selection from their wider literature we can follow something of the course of this debate. We can watch them from their escape from Egypt to the death of their city and beyond. The varied records are here, and the different points of view and changing judgements lie before us. We can see here how men begin to ask religious

---

[1] For the Jewish community, the proper commentary on the Old Testament is *The Mishnah* (translated by H. Danby and published by O.U.P.). 'The Mishnah marks the passage to Judaism as the New Testament marks the passage to Christianity', p.xiii.

[2] See p.22.

questions—and that real religious questions are not merely academic questions. If we read what they have left us properly (and here again we owe it to the scholars that we can do so), we can see within the confines of this small world what such questions involve and why men cannot escape asking them. We can listen to the quiet confidence of the Twenty third Psalm or the cynical poetry of *Ecclesiastes* or the agonized words of *Job*. We can study the varied answers and note the rough edges and the unanswered questions. To say the least, this is a liberal education.

This is not the place to set out the debate—it is not the summary of it but the actual debate itself with its rough edges that must be read for its importance to be grasped. But it is worthwhile, I think, to show that still this Old Testament debate itself is held by important thinkers as deserving careful appraisal. Since the idea that the Old Testament is 'mumbo-jumbo' seems widespread among young people (and others who ought to know better), it is important for the teacher to realize what competent thinkers still have to say about it.

It would be surprising to many young people I meet to find that a thinker of European stature like C.F. von Weizsäcker, lecturing to university audiences on the relevance of science and dealing with the themes of creation and cosmogony, devotes some important pages to analysing and discussing what he calls 'the solemn lucidity of *Genesis* I' and describing the opening stories of that book as 'a true picture of the world'. A teacher should read those Gifford Lectures. [1] And here is George Steiner, discussing what the word 'culture' should mean and surveying the holocaust of Jews on the continent, so different from other earlier massacres, such as those of the Gypsies or the Armenians 'in its idiom of hatred'. He goes on:

Hitler's jibe that 'conscience is a Jewish invention' provides the clue. To speak of the 'invention' of monotheism is to use words in a most provisional way. The cast of intellect, the social forms, the linguistic conventions which accompany the change, maybe in,the oasis of Kadesh, from polytheism to the Mosaic concept of one God, are beyond recall. We cannot feel our way into the minds and skins of men and women who, evidently under constraint and amid frequent rebellion, passed into a new mapping of the world. The immensity of the event, its occurrence in real time, are certain, and reverberate still. The light curves towards us from across the remotest horizon . . . The abruptness of the Mosaic revelation, the

[1] *The Relevance of Science*, pp.47, 53.

finality of the creed at Sinai tore up the human psyche by its most ancient roots. The break has never really knit. [1]

Here indeed—and not from quarters that would naturally suggest themselves—comes an appreciation of the importance of what the Old Testament records. This is the atmosphere in which its insights are to be assessed.

And here again—in a review by Desmond Shawe-Taylor in *The Sunday Times* [2] of Sir Michael Tippett's Third Symphony—is another reminder of the 'relevance' of the Old Testament:

> What is it (the Third Symphony) all about? Nothing less than the Book of Job up to date; the eternal problem, as it now faces us, of Good and Evil; and the guilt felt by the happy in a world of appalling tragedy and sorrow. The idea arose, Sir Michael tells us, from a remark made to him by Colin Davis after a successful performance of (Beethoven's) Ninth Symphony: in effect, 'What can all this out-burst of Joy mean to *us*, now?'

The great debate indeed, in Steiner's words, is an attempt to 'remap the world'. Could its theme be better stated than in this paragraph from a recent book, *An Introduction to the Study of Man*, by Professor J.Z. Young, an outstanding scientist and a Fellow of the Royal Society:

> It is a paradox that although we are still ignorant and feeble our chief problem is to learn to live with our power. We have learned how to destroy each other and even perhaps the whole earth. We have begun to understand our brains so that we can no longer rely on old beliefs to organize society, but we have not learned how to do it afresh . . . Man needs to find out all that he can about himself and the world if he is to survive.

and again

> . . . Man learns and teaches more than any other creature and therefore has the greatest possibility and opportunity to direct the course of events in the world. It is his nature and his biological function or duty to do so. Looking at the whole sequence of the living world there is no doubt of this special position of man . . . There is no need for this pre-eminence to make us arrogant, still less heedless of the significant parts that are played by other organisms. We certainly cannot afford to do so, for we depend on them—are indeed all one with them together. Everything we find about living things emphasizes our unity . . . It is difficult to exaggerate our interdependence. We need plants, animals and bacteria just as they need us. [3]

[1] *Bluebeard's Castle*, pp.35—6.   [2] 25.6.72.

[3] pp. 12, 640 f. A full and comprehensive statement a teacher should consult. The work of another scientist, A.R. Peacocke's *Science and the Christian Experiment*, is also worth reading as a twentieth-century statement of what I have called 'debate and clue'.

Who first raised that kind of question and saw something of its implications?

When we turn to the New Testament, we find ourselves in a different world. Nothing makes this clearer than to note that while there is no real word for 'hope' in the Old Testament (the words it uses are much nearer to 'trust' or 'waiting'), [1] the correspondence of Paul is crowded, we might say, with the word. There is a lively sense in the New Testament (rightly or wrongly) that the questions asked in the Old Testament have received an answer and that the clue to the answer is the life and death and resurrection of Jesus and the new experience of God's love which his followers claimed to have. Whether this answer satisfies us is our own affair; here is the statement of it that is worth our serious consideration. Again the scholars have enabled us to sort out the documents; and again we feel that we are in touch with a living community. Again there are many voices, and again we are enabled to see men beginning to think out afresh all the great questions which the Old Testament raised—and which, indeed, the experiences of all peoples raise.

In these days when these very questions are being widely asked and discussed by young people, stirred into protest by the suffering of small countries and the inhumanity of man to man, here is the classic statement of their protest and a profounder analysis of what is at stake than they are often able to achieve. What touches them most deeply is here seen to be the theme of the poetry of the prophets and of the parables and poetry of Jesus. But it is set against the living story of a people and the life and death of a young man.

As foundation documents

Fourthly, there is a further stage in dealing with the Bible.

Whatever shortcomings the organized institutions of Judaism and Christianity may have, the Jewish community and the Christian community (drawing their boundaries in the widest possible way) are influential communities in the modern world. We have only to think of what we call 'The Jewish Question' and the millions of Jews who have died or been murdered in this century and the emergence of Israel to see how important is the place the Jews have to play in the whole life

[1] Walter Zimmerli, *Man and his Hope in the Old Testament.*

of the world. The Christian community, too, with its new self-awareness as a world fellowship, is profoundly involved in the life of this modern world—the names of Albert Schweitzer, Martin Luther King and Dietrich Bonhoeffer are enough to suggest the varied nature of its influence.

The Bible contains the foundation documents of these two faiths and communities: the Old Testament is the foundation documents of the Jewish people; both Testaments are the foundation documents of the Christian community. If any member of these communities (or any outsider) wants to know what sort of communities these should be, what kind of work and witness they should be concerned about, in a word, who they are, here in these documents is to be found their charter. Both communities have cherished them, not simply as historical accounts of their origins, but as standards by which they judge themselves and are prepared to be judged by others.

As 'my history'

Finally, the Bible is more than literature, the record of great minds, the first great debate about God and the clue, the foundation documents of two significant twentieth century communities. Just because it is all these, it is a religious document in its own right which speaks directly to the serious reader.

The other approaches to the Bible are essential disciplines—they are not 'frills'. The Bible is a down-to-earth book, and we need to know what kind of book we are reading. But the real reason for reading the Bible is that in and through it the reader is made more aware, more sensitive to the whole range of human experience and therefore more aware of what 'being open to the presence of God' means. If God communicates himself to men (as the men and women of the Bible assert) he does so where they are; if he communicates himself to men and women now, he does so through their twentieth century experience. What the Bible does is to light up the whole situation of communication and help us to listen now.

It should be read, not because it is interesting or important history, but because it is a book which enables a reader to learn how to think and live religiously in the world in which he is now living.

What the Bible gives us, if we read it seriously, is a sense of direction.

It looks at the real world we live in, with its passions and senseless
hatreds, its visions and its courage, and it holds on to the conviction
that only faith in a God who is Lord of history and nature and Father
of men and women makes sense of the whole story. It does this not by
speculation but by telling the story of people who faced the worst that
human experience can expose men to, who sought to make sense of it
so that they could live as free men and with joy, and who were content
only with a faith that men could live by. I would agree with Gregor
Smith: 'The biblical tradition is nothing in itself. It would be a double
fatality if we regarded ourselves as forced into a position where we had
merely to reiterate the attitudes and thought-forms of the Bible . . . To
attempt a simple imitation, or representation, of their modes and styles
is to succumb to the pathetic form of the literalist heresy. There is no
way of returning to the world of the Bible. The only possible way
forward is to learn from the biblical writers and then to go our own
way.' [1]

The Bible says to us: this is what the world is really like; this is what
God is like; this is the kind of person you are. This is the direction in
which to look; if you walk in this direction you will find your way.

Realising what kind of book it is

We need, now, to go a step further, and look in more detail at the
form in which the writings of both the Old and New Testaments have
come down to us. I cannot emphasize too clearly that if we are to read
the Bible properly or handle it properly in the classroom, we must keep
clearly in mind what kind of literature we are dealing with. We can
seriously misread it, if we don't.

The Bible is a far more varied book than most people imagine.
Behind the Old Testament lie a thousand years and more of the stormy
history of a small country. Behind the New Testament, the story of a
few generations of what the Roman government considered an underground and subversive movement—small communities meeting in the
back streets of the great Hellenistic cities of the Mediterranean world
who traced their origin back (as their nickname 'Christians' indicated)
to one 'Christus who suffered the extreme penalty during the reign of

---

[1] *The Doctrine of God*, pp.60 f.

Tiberius at the hands of one of our procurators, Pontius Pilatus'. [1]

The Old Testament and the New Testament, as we now have them, are religious selections from a wider literature, and the arrangement they now have is that which seemed most effective for the needs of the communities for whom they were prepared. They grew out of the life of people. Letters were written, documents drawn up, histories made, prophetic poetry born and declaimed, visions recorded, stories remembered as among all peoples. When the selections were made, much was discarded; what was kept was edited and arranged to meet the needs (for the Old Testament) of the Jewish synagogues and (for the New Testament) of the small scattered Christian communities in their worship and teaching. But it is just because they have been selected from a living literature, that we can see beyond the actual collections the outline of the story which really gave them birth. Whatever religious affirmations are set forth in this literature, they have been achieved the hard way; they are not abstract speculations but the living convictions of men and women who have faced the worst and learned how to deal with it.

We turn, then, to look at the story which lies behind the two parts of the Bible. It is a down-to-earth story—this is its strength. It is because it is a particular story about a particular people at a particular period of human history, that it can become, as poets and artist have always seen, the story of Everyman—a classic account of the enduring human predicament.

THE OLD TESTAMENT

The story which lies behind the Old Testament begins about the year 1250 B.C E. with a few thousand conscript labourers in the Delta of the Nile Valley.

We know little of what happened in the centuries before the story begins, but the Israelites always carried with them the memory that they had once been homeless wanderers ('Hebrews') in the Fertile Crescent, the circle of land that rings the great Arabian desert from the Euphrates and Tigris valleys in the north-east to the Nile valley in the south-west.

The story begins with the making of the people out of scattered

[1] Tacitus. D. Ayerst and A.S.T. Fisher, *Records of Christianity*, p. 2.

tribes, and then moves inexorably on, through the making of the nation and the quarrel between North and South, to the extinction of their national life and the story of their survival.

About 1250 B.C.E., we find two groups of Israelite tribes: one group settled in Palestine in the Shechem highlands and in the Negeb in the south; the other group settled in Egypt in the Nile Delta. It is this latter group that concerns us first of all.

The tribes in Egypt had been living there for some time as resident-aliens. At the time the story opens, they had been conscripted as forced labourers by the Egyptian government and set to work on building imperial cities.

The story begins with the escape of a few thousand labourers, under the leadership of Moses, across the Egyptian frontiers, and their skirmishes with border guards. They were a mixed company, for other labourers beside Israelite tribesmen took the opportunity of escaping. Then followed their trek across the desert, their meeting at the Mountain, their rallying at Kadesh Oasis, their march to the Jordan River and their settlement in the highlands of Palestine where they joined up with kinsmen already there.

Here, in the highlands, we find them organized in a loose tribal league associated with a common central shrine (Shechem at first, and then Shiloh). Each tribe—or local group of tribes—still went its own way, for communication between the tribes was difficult; they were divided from one another by the fortified cities of the Esdraelon Valley and by the Canaanite fortress of Jerusalem. Yet they all recognised that they were one people.

About 1100 B.C.E., their very existence was threatened by the landing of some of the Sea Peoples on the plains between the highlands and the sea. These were the Philistines who gave their name to Palestine. They were highly trained soldiers, driven out of the Greek Islands by fierce northern invaders and seeking a homeland along the coast of the eastern Mediterranean. They came armed with iron chariots and iron weapons, attacking the coasts from their high-prowed boats and landing their women and children in ox-carts. They were the first representatives in Palestine of the new Iron Age (the Israelite names for 'knife' and 'helmet' come from Philistine words). [1] They organized

[1] William Culican, *The First Merchant Venturers*, pp. 67 f.

themselves as a league of five cities, and set out to be masters not only of the plains where they landed but of the hills that looked down on them. The Israelites faced defeat.

Two commanders saved them—the brave but erratic Saul and the more far-seeing David. But they did so only at a price.

Saul found out, in the brief and tragic years of his kingship, that a loosely-organized tribal league, with its precarious loyalties, was no match for the better equipped and disciplined Five Cities. He died in battle.

David took a bold step. Not all Israelite tribes belonged to the tribal league. He would bring all Israelite tribes together and really make them one people. But he would do more. Inspired by the vision of Moses, he would build a new nation of Israelites, Philistines and Canaanites as 'God's People', with a professional army and a central government, but centred on the Israelite worship of the God who led them out of Egypt and the covenant he had made with them on the Mountain.

For a few years the Israelites enjoyed their hour of glory; they became the most powerful small nation in the Middle East. The two great empires of Egypt and Assyria were both preoccupied with their own family troubles; their weakness gave David his chance.

But the hour of their glory was a brief one. King David had to face an almost insuperable difficulty—the rift between Israelite and Israelite. The southern Israelites and the northern Israelites were deeply suspicious of one another—perhaps because the latter had been in Egypt and the others had not. He had to face two rebellions against his authority and his policy, first in the south and then in the north. His son, Solomon, who came to the throne as a result of a palace plot, held North and South together only by strong miliary control. At his death the North revolted. The 'one people' of Moses' vision were now two independent nations, sometimes even at war with one another.

The event that crushed them was the rise to immense power of Assyria in the north-east. Its armies marched westward, coveting the wealth of the seafaring cities of Tyre and Sidon on the Mediterranean coast and of Egypt in the south. The two small Israelite kingdoms lay across their path; their fate was inescapable. They perished with the other small kingdoms of Palestine, the North in 722 and the South in

586 (to the Babylonian successor state; the Assyrian capital city, Nineveh, had fallen to Babylonian rebels in 612).

These are the bare bones of the story, as the records bear witness. But nowhere in those records will you find the story told just like this. For, in the minds of the Israelites themselves—the Israelites who survived this story—the events themselves, which they never pretended were anything other than an immense disaster, were not the most important matter. What they were concerned with was not the story itself—who would want to record such humiliation and defeat?—but the meaning of the story. Here their greatest men saw the predicament of humanity and believed that they had discerned its universal meaning.

There were many who saw in it no meaning at all; all that could be done was to put up with it and make the best of it. Wasn't their fate the fate of all small nations? Others became cynical. But others were compelled to ask ultimate questions about the meaning of human existence. How do men live in such a world? What, after all, is worth living for? Is a good world only the wild dream of fanatics? Are burning villages and occupying armies the last word in human history? Is violence all? The real story for historian and prophet alike—the historians who wrote down, from such records as they had, what had happened as a cautionary tale, and the prophets who inspired their vision and directed their judgment—was the story of their faith, a faith which could survive political extinction and even take some of them back, after the 586 disaster, to rebuild the city and begin life again.

THE NEW TESTAMENT

The world of the New Testament is a small world indeed though the background against which it is set is that of the Roman Empire itself. The story that lies behind it is the story of a few thousand people and it covers only a few decades.

The New Testament itself consists of documents that arose out of the life and worship of the small Christian communities: 'gospels' which are at once narratives and more than narratives about their Founder and Lord, Jesus of Nazareth; and letters which are real letters (unlike the literary letters of the day) but dealt with matters of the Christian faith and practice. But behind the gospels and letters can be seen something of the dramatic story out of which they were written. It is the story of

one man—three brief public years, his execution in 29 C.E. outside his
capital city, and his profound influence over his friends (Christians had
their own explanation of this remarkable influence) and, through them,
on a widening circle who were bound together in a new fellowship
which was both their surprise and joy, and which they described as
being 'one in Christ' (to use their own words), where 'there was no
question of Greek and Jew, circumcised and uncircumcised (religious
differences), barbarian, Scythian, freeman, slave; but Christ is all, and
is in all'. [1]

If it were not for one book—the second part of Luke's account of
the origin and spread of the Christian community (*The Gospel
according to Luke*, and *The Acts of the Apostles*, parts one and two
of one work)—we should know little of the next thirty years, except
what can be gleaned from Paul's correspondence. Even Luke gives us
only a small and highly selective account.

In a sense, much as we would like to know about the persons
involved in the story and their travels and activities, such events were
not the concern either of the writers or of the communities to which
they belonged. What is set out in letter and gospel is their conviction
that the brief story of Jesus and the fellowship of his friends which
was growing and spreading throughout the known world was the climax
of the whole story which lies behind the Old Testament. They felt that
they were writing the last chapter of that long story and the first chapter of the story of a new age. The real story here is not that of their
own activities, but that of Jesus—chiefly his death and his defeat of
death (they were not followers of a dead teacher but of a living Lord,
they believed). Here in this story the questions which the dark experience of the Israelites had raised and the convictions which had begun
to make sense of their experience received, for them, a final and
unambiguous answer. What they proclaim—and the New Testament is
very much of a proclamation—is the brief but vital climax of the story
which began with the escape from Egypt so long ago and even before.
Hence the dominance of a new note of joy and hope, the claim that
ordinary people can now live 'more splendidly than the greatest world-
conquerors' and the assertion that the death of Jesus—which would

---

[1] Col. 3. 11 (*New World*, 307).

have seemed a brutal execution to an onlooker (deserved or undeserved, according to your point of view)—was something to glory in.

MORE THAN A STORY

It will now be obvious that though behind the whole of the Bible there is a real story about real people which can be seen in sufficient detail for us to know what kind of story it is, there is in the Bible much more than a story. There is an exploration of the human predicament in all its stark reality; the writers see in the story of the Israelite people and in the story of Jesus a key to the mystery of all human experience and a way to make sense of what actually is happening in our world. Whether they are right or wrong is for every man to judge for himself; this is their claim.

But they do not make it as a wild guess. They lived too near the agony of suffering to be interested in guesses. After all, the central events of their story are the death of a city and the death of a young man. But they had clues. For the Israelites it was the escape of a handful of slaves out of Egypt; for the Christians it was the life and death of Jesus as they saw it in the light of their later experience. How they used these events as clues cannot be easily summarised; but their reasons—which are cogent reasons—only really become clear as we immerse ourselves in the records which they have left us—read and reread their story until we 'can hear them talking' (as one historian has said we should read the history of a people).

This, then, is the kind of book we are dealing with. Whatever else we do with it in the classroom, we must not water it down.

Its theme

Before we go any further, let us stand back and ask if there is any predominant theme which gives all this varied literature a compelling unity, an underlying motif which we can keep in mind while we deal with particular incidents in the developing story or particular aspects of the developing argument. It is very important, as I shall say later, always to be aware of 'the sweep of the story' and to keep it constantly in mind. And by 'sweep of the story' I am not thinking of any artificial structuring of the documents that lie before us, but what naturally emerges as a deepening and persistent concern. One aspect of the

sweep of the story is what I have called 'the story which lies behind
the two Testaments'; the other I come to now—the increasing consensus
of judgment towards which the profoundest minds of the Israelite
people move.

'It is possible,' writes John Austin Baker, 'to find without falsification one
theme running through this collection (of both Testaments), even if not instanced
in every part. What this then is as regards the Old Testament . . . (can be) summarised as the attempt to see all existence in terms of the sovereignty of God, and to
define Man's place in that overall scheme. The unifying key to the Old Testament,
therefore, is its great fundamental question, not its answers, explicit or implied.
It might be considered frivolous, but it would not be far from the truth to say
that the question is in fact the only thing which the Old Testament does get right,
and that the answers, at least in their Old Testament form, are all wrong. But in
the end it is the question that matters, for it is this question which is answered
correctly in Jesus; and it was because Israel was the only nation that did ask this
question that God incarnate had to be a Jew. In no other setting would his life
have made any sense. The New Testament writers in their turn, therefore, are
able to communicate and interpret God's own answer because, through the
medium of Judaism, they shared the question. But had the cross and resurrection
of Jesus not made that answer so clear and definite, they would never have
realized that Israel's own ancient answers were inadequate. As it was, however,
they were able, as Paul for example so often did, to bring out new truth by
contrasting it with the old mistakes—though some of them . . . at times found
the gravitational field of those mistaken systems too strong for them.' [1]

Here then is what I have called the Great Debate and the Clue. Is
there any motif which links both debate and clue together and provides the real reason for seeing them both (as most Christians have
always done) as sharing a common awareness? Is there a deeply
spiritual link between the two, something other than an obvious
historical one? Let us take each Testament by itself.

The Old Testament

Two quotations will help us to see what the deeper theme of the
Old Testament was.

The first is a 'Confession of Faith'. It may be very old, though it
comes to us in the form in which we now have it, from *Deuteronomy*,
that radical revision of Israelite life and worship undertaken not long
before the final disaster of the fall of Jerusalem.

[1] *The Foolishness of God*, p. 362.

At the Harvest Festival in Jerusalem, the Israelite farmers brought baskets filled with some of the produce of their fields. As they offered these gifts to God, they were each required to say these words:

My ancestors were a small company of homeless nomads who entered Egypt and lived there as resident-aliens. We became a strong and large tribe. The Egyptians gave us a hard time, treated us brutally and forced us to work as slave labourers. We appealed to GOD, our ancestral God. He took note of us and saw what a brutal life we were forced to live as slaves. He rescued us with terrifying deeds of violent strength—with many signs and wonders—and led us here to this rich and fertile land of ours. Look! I bring this harvest of the soil which you, O GOD, have given me. [1]

These words may have meant to many farmers no more than 'The land is ours now!' But for the men who drew this up as part of the Harvest Worship they meant much more. They were meant to make clear that, for the Israelite people, the most important thing in their history was not their military exploits but GOD's love given to men who had no claim on him or anyone else. Why should a handful of slaves conscripted for the building of Egyptian cities (so runs their argument) be loved by God? Over the years this thought deepened into the conviction of God's love for all mankind—'He led the Philistines from Crete, and the Syrians from beyond Damascus', as well as the Israelites from Egypt. [2]

The second quotation brings this conviction of God's love out into the open:

GOD is my shepherd:
> I shall lack nothing;
>> he lets me lie down on green grass,
> leads me by quiet streams,
>> makes me a new man.
> He guides me along the right tracks
>> because he is what he is;
> when I go through the pitch-black gorge
>> nothing frightens me.

> You are with me,
>> club and staff at the ready—
>> making me strong!

[1] 189
[2] 244

> You are my host, I am your guest
>   while my enemies look helplessly on!
> You bathe my head with oil,
>   fill my cup to the brim!
>
> Your goodness and love shall follow me
>   all my days!
> GOD's home is my home
>   for ever! [1]

These are words that can be said by anybody—Israelite and foreigner alike; so they have been said all over the world and throughout the centuries since they were written.

The theme of the Old Testament is then, not the defeat of a small nation (which seems so easily on a first reading to be its ostensible theme) but God's 'steadfast love'. This conviction was not a wild or desperate cry, but a real conviction won in the face of the stubborn and frightening facts of their stormy and humiliating experience. This is what it was all about; this is something a man can live by and in the light of which he can make sense of the strange world in which he is living; this is true for all men everywhere whoever they are. The Israelites did not see it in all its clarity; they did not understand all its implications; they did not work out all its wide-ranging meaning. But they saw it, and their most serious people, whether famous prophet or humble farmer, lived by it.

The New Testament

If 'steadfast love' (*chesed*) is the great word of the Old Testament, 'love' (*agape*) is the undoubted word for the New Testament. Jesus himself did not use the word much, except when he was quoting or referring to the Old Testament; but its nature is the theme of his stories and poems. The pages of Paul's letters and the Fourth Gospel are crowded with it; one of Paul's most famous statements (1 Cor. 13) is an exposition of it with what looks like a thumb-nail sketch of the character of Jesus at the heart of it. [2] It is not the dictionary meaning of the word that matters (although it seems as if the first Christians minted it to express their new awareness) but the way in which this

---

[1] 386
[2] *NW* 319 f.

word is given its immense meaning by all that Jesus was and said and by
the new experience of God he made possible.

Three quotations here will suffice. The first is from Jesus himself:

> Don't worry about what you are going to eat
>   or what sort of clothes you are going to wear;
> what you are is more important than what you eat,
>   what you are is more important that what you wear.
>
> Look at the wild birds:
>   they don't go out farming;
>   they have no store-house or barn;
> God feeds them.
>   How much more than wild birds you mean to God!
>
> Look at the wild flowers:
>   they don't work like mothers at home.
> Yet believe me, King Solomon wasn't robed as gloriously
>   as a wild flower.
>
> God dresses the wild grass—
>   blowing in the field today,
>   a bonfire on the farm tomorrow.
>
> How much more will God look after you!
>   You don't trust him enough. [1]

And here is Paul writing:

We know now that the world is not the sort of world we once thought it was.
It is a world where God works for all that is worth-while, *alongside those who
love him*. We are fellow-workers with God. That is what he was always calling us
to be—with one purpose in mind, a purpose he planned and settled before history
began. This purpose was that we might grow up to be the kind of person Jesus
was; so that Jesus might be the elder brother of a great family of brothers and
sisters . . .

Who can take God's love away from us now—the love which Jesus has made
real to us?

You know the sort of thing that can happen to any of us in this world of ours—
suffering, hardship, cruelty, hunger, homelessness, danger, war. In just such a
world, we who are the friends of Jesus can live more splendidly than the greatest
world-conquerors—with the help of Jesus who loved us.

I am quite sure that nothing—neither dying nor living, neither what we're
facing now nor what we may have to face tomorrow, nothing in our own world
or in outer space or in our own hearts—can take away from us God's love, made
real by Jesus our Lord. [2]

[1] *NW* 97.
[2] *NW* 306 f.

The last is from a letter written towards the end of the first century:

> This is how God's love has been made clear to us: he sent his only Son to live among us to help us to live splendidly. I'm not thinking, you see, of the way we love God, but of the way he loves us . . . That is how we know what love means . . .
>
> God is love itself. So, if we live in love—and we can see what this means by remembering how Jesus lives—we live in God's presence and he lives in our hearts. With love like this in our hearts—love for God and love for one another—there's nothing that can ever make us afraid, for such love drives all fear away. You see, God loved us first, and we learned how to love from him. [1]

Anyone who reads the New Testament with any care is quickly aware of this underlying theme. But it is important to see that 'love' gets its meaning from the whole story out of which it emerges. Paul's letters are no academic debate, thrown off as they were in the most crowded ten years of his life—they are an attempt to work out what love means for ordinary men and women involved in the rough encounters of the everyday world; and what, if love is the clue to the universe, is the way we ought to think of the whole range of nature and history. That is why this is the theme of that first comprehensive presentation of the Christian faith, the Fourth Gospel, where the word 'love' is made central.

Neither 'steadfast love' in the Old Testament nor 'love' in the New have a touch of sentimentality about them. The story out of which they have arisen and taken their meaning prevents any glib use of either of them. They are marked too deeply by the suffering and death of many men and women. They stand, not only for a profound understanding of God, but also for a way of living, a way which alone can make our world a really human world. We know today, from our wider experience and from the wide-ranging enquiries of historian and scientist, how much vaster and more wonderful the universe is than the men of the Bible ever knew. But its central question remains the same.

The relevance of the biblical theme may perhaps be high-lighted if the above quotations are put beside another—from the closing pages of the unofficial report commissioned for the Conference on the Human Environment by the Secretary-General of the United Nations and published in 1972:

[1] *NW* 349

With war as mankind's oldest custom and divided sovereignty as his most treasured inheritance, where are the energies, the psychic force, the profound commitment needed for a wider loyalty?

Loyalty, however, may be the key. It is the view of many modern psychologists that man is a killer not because of any biological imperative but because of his capacity for misplaced loyalty. He will do in the name of a wider allegiance what he would shrink to do in his own nature. His massive, organized killings—the kind that distinguish him from all other animals—are invariably done in the name of faith and group of people or clan. And here, it is not wholly irrational to hope that the full realization of planetary interdependence—in biosphere and technosphere alike—may begin to affect man in the depths of his capacity for psychic commitment. All loyalty is based on two elements—the hope of protection and the hope of enhancement. On either count, the new ecological imperative can give a new vision of where man belongs in his final security and his final sense of dignity and identity . . .

Alone in space, alone in its life-supporting systems, powered by inconceivable energies, mediating them to us through the most delicate adjustments, wayward, unlikely, unpredictable but nourishing, enlivening and enriching in the largest degree—is not this a precious home for all of us earthlings? Is it not worth our love? Does it not deserve all the inventiveness and courage and generosity of which we are capable to preserve it from degradation and destruction and, by doing so, to secure our own survival? [1]

After such words, do not Paul's words, written nearly two thousand years ago, sound to the point?

We look at everything differently now—the hard time we are going through and the very earth we live on. We see it all in the light of the glorious future which God will give us.

The earth itself is being spoiled by the way men live; it is, as it were, waiting for the time when the people who live on it will live, not as they do now, but as members of God's Family, with mercy and gentleness, sharing it together . . .

All this, of course, is only a hope now; we don't live as we ought to. But this hope has made us new men. And we're going to hold on until the day comes when we can see it with our own eyes. [2]

Its background

I need not do more than briefly emphasize that no one will really begin to understand the Bible who does not read it against the background of the whole ancient world in which the Israelite kingdoms were a tiny and apparently insignificant, and the early Christian

---

[1] Barbara Ward and René Dubois, *Only One Earth*, p. 296.
[2] *NW* 306.

communities a negligible part. Here the teacher is helped by the many splendid books which have been published in recent years. It is not a learned knowledge of this ancient world he needs, but a sense of its existence and a respect for its importance. If God has never left himself without a witness, what was happening and what was being thought in the surrounding peoples give the Israelite religion its proper setting; what was stirring in the world of Greece and Rome is the illuminating context of Christian worship and thought. Young people, while reading the Bible, should be encouraged to browse in books which picture this wider world.

The biblical writers were profoundly influenced, as we all are, by the events and atmosphere of the world in which they were living. There were always 'isolationists' among them (like the Rechabites of the Old Testament or the author of *Revelation* in the New); but the decisive figures of the Bible lived in their world with 'critical awareness'— borrowing, rethinking, criticizing, renewing, as books like R.E. Clements's *God and Temple* and C.H. Dodd's *The Interpretation of the Fourth Gospel* make very clear.

But, for young people and especially for the teacher in the classroom, I am thinking of something much simpler—the many popular books that have been written by expert historians about the peoples of the Middle East, the spread of Greek culture and life in the Roman Empire. For example, the first part of *Winding Quest* is given a sense of reality (far from the 'David and Goliath' approach) by being read against the wider picture painted in William Culican's *The First Merchant Venturers*; [1] the account of the ministry of Jesus and the travels of Paul are likewise given a new slant if, while we are reading the gospel accounts or *The Acts of the Apostles*, we have beside us Yigael Yadin's magnificently illustrated *Masada* with the light it throws on the Resistance Movement in first-century occupied Palestine [2] and begin to realize the atmosphere in which Jesus lived and the sources of the violence Paul met in Jerusalem and elsewhere.

But it is not only the historical background that matters; the

---

[1] For the Old Testament, the teacher will find Martin Noth's *The Old Testament World* an excellent guide.

[2] Josephus's *The Jewish War* (Penguin Classics) is indispensable reading.

geographical background matters just as much. A feeling for the very country that was their home is a necessary help in seeing the people of the Bible as real people living in a real world. Their lives cannot be abstracted from the physical world that dictated much of the pattern of their daily experience. If we are to read the Bible until we can 'hear people talking', we must have some understanding of what it was like to stand in the Jordan Valley and stare up at the forbidding highlands or look down (as Jesus did) on the wide Esdraelon Valley with its busy traffic.

It was the landscape of their country, the course of the seasons and the succession of wind and rain and sun, the sudden flowers of a brief spring or the withering winds from the desert that gave their poets the imagery of their poetry. Against such a background the imagery of Jesus, in parable and poem suddenly comes to life.

An excellent guide is Denis Baly's *The Geography of the Bible*.

George Adam Smith's classical account, *The Historical Geography of the Holy Land* (now available in paperback), is a book every teacher ought to read; the biblical story and geographical background are unforgettably described.

There is no short cut to the reading of the Bible. If we merely skim through it, we shall hear nothing. The world of the Bible is a living world, and the Bible itself is the legacy of the men and women who lived in it. If we would read it with understanding, we must take the trouble, by an act of the imagination, to 'stand and stare' with them.

Reading it

It is important for the teacher—and the young reader—that he should be familiar with the whole of the Bible, not just the parts of it with which he may be specially concerned or which he judges to be 'the most important passages'.

This means that he should enjoy and take time about his reading. Our common habit (if it is still a habit) is to read limited sections too brief to give any sense of the range of biblical literature. We need to read more widely and to read with a relaxed mind, as we read other literature which we enjoy. The great modern translations here come to our help, with their fresh present-day language, their playing down of chapter and verse (these have nothing to do with the original text), their setting-out of the text with some reference to the natural divisions of what is being translated, and their printing of poetry as poetry (though I wish they would be bolder about this).

As we read, we must keep in mind what kind of book the Bible is, the great variety of literary forms that it contains, and the changing moods which characterize it.

These seventeenth century words should be graven on our minds. They come from one of Benjamin Whichcote's sermons, and they have been quoted, very aptly, to describe the attitude of one of the outstanding biblical scholars of this century: 'The Scripture is to be read as a man would read a letter from a friend, in which he doth only look after what was in his friend's mind and meaning, not what he can put upon his words.' [1]

In the light of the work of biblical scholars

What I have been setting out so far is the way in which I read the Bible, and the steps by which I approach it: as literature, as sitting at the feet of men of profound insight, as the record of the first great debate about the meaning of religion (its nature and its clue), as the foundation documents of the community of which I am a member, and as the chief way (this is my experience) of helping me to clarify my own experience and deepen my awareness of God's presence. So far, so good. But I have been assuming that we are reading the full text of the Bible as we find it in the fine modern translations—the whole two thousand pages of such editions, beginning at *Genesis* and ending with *Revelation.* And I have talked about reading it 'properly' and 'seriously'. I come now to say something about what I have so far only hinted at or implied: that to do this we need to read the Bible in the light of modern study and research; and that we need to take this research much more seriously than we do, in both the reading and the teaching of the Bible.

There is no doubt that, if you have the background knowledge and unflagging interest, the reading of the whole full text can be immensely rewarding and enlightening. My grandfather was a Methodist Local Preacher in north Staffordshire. I was only a boy when he died, but I

---

[1] J.T. Wilkinson, *Arthur Samuel Peake: A Biography*, p. 92.

remember, when staying with him, a group of men who used to meet in his kitchen to study the Bible and went on talking long into the night. I could hear them from my bedroom above the kitchen and I used to wonder what they were talking about. I knew from the way my grandfather used to talk to me how much the Bible meant to him, and I was to learn later how much his wisdom and Christian understanding mattered in the life of that mining village. When his Bible came into my hands at his death, I could see by the stained pages that, deeply conservative about biblical matters as he was, he had made his own selection—*Genesis, Isaiah* and *Jeremiah* and the Book of *Psalms*, the Gospels (especially *John*) and *Romans* were stained dark. He had used his own evangelical experience as his guide. He had learned much (as I could tell from his sermon notes). But the Bible is a far bigger and profounder book than his evangelical theology allowed him to see; it is far bigger than all theological and ecclesiastical points of view of modern biblical scholars.

The study of modern biblical scholars who have made clear how profound the insights of the Bible are, is now public knowledge, and their work (of which my grandfather knew little and of which, if he had known about it, he would probably have disapproved) is talked about on the television and radio and in the newspapers, and is to be found on the shelves of public libraries, open to all. This work rests on the assumption (a very right one) that the sources of all our knowledge and convictions need critical examination if what we profess to believe is not to degenerate into superstition or mere party propaganda or wishful thinking.

If we are to read the Bible and our reading is to mean anything to us, we must read it in the light of the most thorough critical examination that is available and in the light of all we know about its sources and content and background, as historian and archaeologist, literary critic and theologian have disentangled and unfolded it.

But here is the snag for young people and for the busy teacher in the classroom: the full text lies before us, magnificently translated; the research of scholars is embodied in books (many written—and excellently written—to guide the ordinary reader) on the bookshelves of the libraries; how does the untrained reader (and it needs very special training to find your way) read the one in the light of the other?

It is this, I think, almost more than anything else, which accounts for the fact that, as Dr. Busia says in his *Urban Churches in Britain*, 'the Bible seems virtually to have ceased to be the "food" of the Church. Even for those who are regular Church members, the Bible seems to have lost its relevance to their daily lives'—and this on the evidence of what the members themselves said. [1]

If adults—and members of the Christian Church themselves have found it difficult to read the Bible with a sense of relevance, how much more can young people with little or no experience of Christian worship or Church fellowship, be forgiven for thinking it 'boring' and saying 'the older you get, the less you think of the Bible'. [2]

It is to meet the needs of young people like this that *New World* and *Winding Quest* were made. We can now turn to what I have tried to do there.

[1] p. 132.
[2] Quoted by Harold Loukes in *Teenage Religion*.

CHAPTER TWO

WORKING IT OUT

Language and Comprehension

The making of *New World* began, as it were, in the classroom, with
the demand of some of my students and some practising teachers for a
simple translation of the biblical text for use with pupils for whom
reading did not come easily; and since it was the story of Jesus with
which students were most often asked to deal, we began with Mark's
gospel. It was soon obvious that it was not only simple language that
was needed. If they were to understand the story they were reading,
the full text of the Bible needed to be simplified and rearranged. This
was especially true when we went on to deal with the teaching of Jesus.

The first two parts of *New World–The Beginning* and *The Message–*
aimed at a reading age of about 9 years. *From Galilee to Rome* keeps
within the same range but with a somewhat enlarged vocabulary. In
Paul the Explorer and *Jesus–Leader and Lord*, where we are dealing
with Paul's correspondence and 'the first comprehensive statement of
the Christian Faith', the Fourth Gospel, 12 years reading age is aimed
at; for here questions are raised which can only properly be dealt with
in the secondary school when young people have passed what Ronald
Goldman has called 'the marked watershed in religious thinking', about
the age of 13. Here both Paul and the author of the Fourth Gospel are
tackling that rethinking of our fundamental assumptions about Man
and God which taking Jesus seriously demands; they are looking at the
implications of Christian experience.

When I came to deal with the Old Testament, which I am convinced
should only be seriously tackled with young people who have begun to
look critically at the world we are living in and to ask questions about
our fundamental assumptions, I aimed again at a reading age of about
12 years. In the first three parts of *Winding Quest–Brief Hour of Glory*,
Memories of the Past and *The Death of Two Cities* (which in a way
correspond to the first three parts of *New World*)–I was able to keep
the vocabulary within limits. In the last two parts–*Making Sense of*

the Story and *Enduring Convictions*—where we are dealing, to a large extent, with prophetic speech and dramatic poetry such as we find in *Job* and *Ecclesiastes*, I let the rich vocabulary of the poetry have more of its own way.

I have not worked with a word-list, though I have consulted and used such research as is contained in Dr. D.G. Burns's *The Vocabulary of the Secondary Modern School Child* and R.P.A. Edwards and Vivian Gibbon's *Words Your Children Use*. I have discussed with practising teachers the linguistic difficulties met in the classroom and I have talked with young people themselves. I have read through much of *Winding Quest* with a group of adults and young people. All through I have tried to keep sentences simple and short.

My hardest problem was to make the translation sound adult, and, as far as possible, look adult. I am greatly indebted to the many groups of adults (in the earlier stages, unsuspecting groups) to whom I have read the translation. With *Winding Quest*, I have been able to read many parts of it to larger groups of adults and young people and to benefit by the lively discussions which followed.

Nothing could be more disastrous than 'writing down' to young people; I think we often under-estimate the abilities of slower readers to grasp what the great human questions the Bible raises are about and to discuss them with insight and intelligence.

But, if they are to understand what they are reading and be able to see the Bible as a whole, they need more than the help of simple language. So I have given a selection of biblical material to help them to follow the central theme; and even within this selection of material I have had to simplify and sometimes paraphrase.

Certain parts cried out for simplification: for example, Baruch's rather prosy story about Jeremiah and his speeches I have drastically paraphrased. But I have been compelled to paraphrase many of the selections from Paul's letters and (most regrettably) the conversations in the Fourth Gospel where I had to simplify if such passages were to be handled meaningfully in the classroom at all. I have done what I could to keep it within bounds. I have checked myself by submitting my version to others far more competent than I am, and I have been glad to accept their suggestions and criticisms. Within these limits, additions to the text and omissions from it have been kept as few as

possible; and in paraphrasing I have kept, as far as possible, to the
wording of the writers themselves, only on occasions using a phrase
from a scholar whose summary of a difficult paragraph seemed to me
the most accurate way in which I could give it. [1] I have nowhere added
anything of substance. My additions are what I consider to be legitimate
extensions of my method of translation; they are really only forms of
paraphrase—necessary information, simple explanations of linking
phrases. I have omitted passages which I judged to be beyond the grasp
of young people at this stage or where the issue would require more
comment to make clear than I could allow myself (e.g. Jesus's discussion of divorce, and *Mark* 13).

Hence, in my selection and simplication of material and in whatever
paraphrase I felt necessary to venture, I have followed the biblical
scholars as my guides and set out what I have called 'the heart' of the
Old and New Testaments as they themselves broadly see it. I wanted
to be able to say 'This is what the Bible is about; there is much more in
it which one day I hope you will read and think about—but this only
deepens or develops or discusses what you will find here; this is the
heart of the Bible'.

I have had to come down on one side of the fence or the other, of
course, where there is still debate among competent men. But I have
done so openly; for I think it an excellent venture for a teacher who
disagrees with my judgment to discuss the whole matter, as he thinks
fit, with the young people themselves. They should know that there
is a debate, and that the task of understanding the Bible is not something that can be done once and for all. Each age takes the study
further and learns from the achievements and mistakes of those who
have gone before them; each age asks different questions, has different
concerns and faces different social situations; and therefore has to look
afresh at what we have learned and are still learning about the past,
and survey it from a different angle. The Bible, itself part of the history
of our past, is not exempt from this continuing scrutiny. New discoveries,
new experiences and the new perspectives they make possible demand
this continuing re-examination. So young people in the classroom—and
ordinary readers reading it for themselves—should be made aware of

[1] See *NW* p.306 where I use a phrase from Professor C.F.D. Moule's summary
of the argument: 'with mercy and gentleness, sharing it together'.

this continuing discussion and be helped to take their part in a living debate.

This, it seems to me, is the only way in which the 'truth' of the Bible can be seen. 'There is only one right way of asking men to believe, which is to put before them what they ought to believe because it is true; and there is only one right way of persuading, which is to present what is true in such a way that nothing will prevent it from being seen except the desire to abide in darkness.'[1]

Arrangement of the Bible

There is one more very important preliminary matter to deal with before we come to the contents of the Bible itself. If the ordinary reader needs help in the simplication of biblical material (in the sense in which I have discussed it), he also needs help with the arrangement of the material. This is true of the New Testament; it is especially true of the Old Testament which has a long and complex literary history and where even a single book or 'roll' (such, for example, as *Isaiah* which is a compendium of many prophetic utterances over perhaps more than five hundred years) can have a complex history of its own.

The arrangement of both Old and New Testaments, as they now lie before us, is a religious arrangement made over the course of either centuries or decades, to meet the specific needs of religious communities: the Old Testament the needs of the Jewish synagogues after the Exile;[2] the New Testament the needs of the Christian churches towards the end of the second century C.E. The importance of this arrangement is clear; it sets out the unifying convictions of the Jewish and Christian communities which gather up and transcend the varieties of individual attitude and utterance to be found within their writings. There is a common vision (I prefer the word 'vision' to the commonly used word 'theology' here) which crowns the varied documents of each Testament with its own authority and which accounts for the actual selection which was made.

But this very order, clear enough to the communities who made it, is a real hindrance to the ordinary reader today, who wants to begin at

[1] John Oman, *Grace and Personality*, p. 143.

[2] Not finally settled until about 90 C.E. when the last part of the Old Testament was agreed upon. For Jesus the Scripture was still just 'the Law and the Prophets'.

the beginning and go on to the end, as he does with other books he
reads. What impresses him if he plods on (most don't) is not a unity of
vision but a hotch-potch of the strangest kind; whatever 'vision' there
may be here he has to take for granted and at second-hand. He cannot
see it for himself. So he lives, not in the whole territory of, say, the
Bible, but in isolated areas, the Book of *Psalms* or *The Gospel according
to St. John*, as my grandfather did. How these lie within a wider story
and why they should lie cheek by jowl with documents like *Leviticus*
or *Chronicles* or *Revelation* he has no clue. If he is to take his first
steps in reading the Bible with intelligence and understanding (as I
have said, it is *reading* the Bible, not *reading about* it, that matters),
he needs to approach it in a very different way. It is important for him
to know that in opening the Bible and reading its first two chapters he
is passing from the fifth century B.C.E. back five hundred years to
the tenth century; or that when he passes from the reading of *Luke* to
the reading of *John* he is turning to a different kind of account of the
ministry of Jesus.

The arrangement of the New Testament, made over the comparatively
short period of about a hundred and fifty years, presents fewer difficulties to the beginner than the Old Testament does. Its pattern of
Gospel—Acts—Letters marks a proper approach. The story of Jesus is
at the heart of it; what happened to the small communities of his
friends after his death and resurrection naturally follows; the letters
etc. that follow discuss what all this means. But the impression it gives
that *Matthew* is the first and *Revelation* the last document (either in
time or importance) is misleading. That the Fourth Gospel is, in a real
sense, the crown of the New Testament is obscured by the 'four gospel'
pattern. What is more, the sayings of Jesus as his friends reported them
are most difficult to see as a whole; they are now embedded, in varying
versions and arrangements, in the narratives of the gospels. But what
Jesus himself had to say is not a mere appendix to what he did; what
he had to say, even though we only have it in the way his friends
remembered and reported it, is crucial for understanding why he did
what he did. Immense research and study has been given to his sayings;
young people need the help of this study if they are to read the gospels
with real understanding. Nor would they know that *The Gospel
according to St. Luke* and *The Acts of the Apostles* are 'part one' and

'part two' of a single work; and that we best get the feel of how early
Christians began to think out their convictions by moving forward from
the correspondence of Paul to that 'first comprehensive statement of
the Christian Faith', the Fourth Gospel.

When we turn to the Old Testament, some rearrangement of the
documents we find there is essential if young people are to find their
way and begin to understand (instead of just being told) what the Old
Testament is about. Their first steps must not be into the territory of
Genesis if they are not to start asking the wrong questions and making
age-old misjudgments, and being completely beaten when they move
from the impressive stories of *Genesis* and *Exodus* into the complicated
corpus of legal codes which follow them. Yet some acquaintance with
these legal codes is important—religious vision and religious convictions
have to be worked out into the fabric of social life; they have political
implications—and it would be a pity, to say the least, if they never
discovered that remarkable and unique legal document, *Deuteronomy*.
For the 'laws' of the Bible are not a permanent common law of human
society (yet note how often the 'Ten Commandments' are still taught
with this assumption). They remind us how religious insights have to
mould the stubborn legacy of human institutions which every generation
inherits, and the pitfalls and dangers in the way.

The pattern of the Old Testament was settled over about five hundred
years. Its three parts have a real logic about them. The first, 'Torah'
('Religion' rather than 'Law') sets the groundwork of the Israelites'
religious convictions; here is their account of how they became 'God's
People' and what they believed their function in human society was.
'The Prophets' (which includes the great 'History of the People and
their Land'—*Joshua* to *Kings*—as well as the prophetic collections—the
four 'rolls', *Isaiah*, *Jeremiah*, *Ezekiel* and *The Twelve*) is concerned
with the meaning of their history. The last part, 'The Writings', consists
of later writings and includes important books like the *Psalms* and *Job*
and *Daniel*. How is the ordinary reader to find his way here and be
helped to read the Old Testament as the living record it is—as God's
dealings with 'his People' (as Jewish and Christian people would say)?
Only, I am convinced, by some bold rearrangement of the material
which shall at once be true to the original vision of the people who
wrote and collected it together and to the insights and discoveries of

scholarly research which has done so much to bring the Old Testament alive, not simply as an historical account of the Israelite people ('a book full of stories') but as the statement of their faith which has a vital relevance for our twentieth century world.

So this is what I have done.

WINDING QUEST

In *Brief Hour of Glory*, I follow the early source of *Samuel*, in *Memories of the Past* the earlier Judaean source ('J'), in *The Death of Two Cities* a selection of the narratives from *Kings* to show the story moving relentlessly to the final disaster. I have omitted, except in one or two places, all later accounts and editorial comments and expansions. Important as these are at the proper moment, here, at a first reading of the Old Testament, they would only blur the account. For the story of the return and the rebuilding of temple and city, I judged the diary of Nehemiah sufficient. In *Making Sense of the Story*, I give a fairly full account of *Amos*, the whole of Baruch's account of Jeremiah and a selection of Jeremiah's poetry; for the Prophet of the Exile, I give the four 'Servant Poems' and a selection from the others. In *Enduring Convictions*, for *Genesis* I give the later Priestly account of the creation ('P–307'), and for the rest I follow the earliest account ('J'). I give *Ruth* and *Jonah* in full, follow Dr. Snaith's suggestion about the form of the first book of *Job* (which the author later expanded and developed), and give three stories from the first part of *Daniel* and the first Vision (enough to show the structure and argument of the book). For the other books of the Old Testament, I had to be content with a few selections; for the Book of *Psalms*, I was able to follow Dr. Leslie's *The Psalms*, where he translates and arranges the psalms according to their type; I have given psalms from each type (see Appendix A).

NEW WORLD

In *New World*, I give Mark's account of Jesus, since *Mark* is generally reckoned to be the first of the gospels to be written down and gives a vivid picture of how the early Christians remembered what Jesus did and said and how he died. *Matthew*, which is an enlarged edition of *Mark*, can, to begin with, be left on one side. I have given most of *Mark*, following Dr. Vincent Taylor's commentary and

T.W. Manson's *The Servant-Messiah.* For the teaching of Jesus, which
seems to me the most mishandled part of the New Testament, I
followed the commentaries (especially T.W. Manson's *The Teaching of
Jesus*); but arranged the material so that the form of the remembered
sayings can be seen: I give, first, a number of what Dr. Taylor calls
'Pronouncement Stories'—stories remembered because of something
Jesus said; then forty-five of the parables and about forty of Jesus's
poems (I come back later to the question of his poetry). Here sub-
stantially are what the scholars I was following would consider to be
the undoubted sayings of Jesus. In delimiting the parables (which appear
in the synoptic gospels as parts of collections of the sayings of Jesus) I
followed, in addition to Manson, Jeremias's *The Parables of Jesus* and
B.D.T. Smith's *The Parables of the Synoptic Gospels.* This part, therefore, is broadly speaking an edition of 'Q', the suggested early source
of the sayings (oral or written) which lies behind *Matthew* and *Luke.*

It has long been known that the stories about Jesus and the sayings
attributed to him come to us in the versions used in the preaching of
the early Christians. I have followed (again only sufficiently for my
purpose) the units suggested in the study of the gospels known as
Form-History; so that the teacher can, if and when he wishes, use the
units in a discussion with his young people about the question of how
reliable the traditions behind the gospels are. This, at any rate, is what
they remembered and how they reported what they remembered.

It has always seemed a great pity that while scholars have long held
that *The Gospel of Luke* and *The Acts of the Apostles* are part one and
part two of an account of the origins and convictions of the Christian
community, most people read them and teachers deal with them as
separate works. Their separation took place when the New Testament's
structure was being worked out in the latter half of the second century.
Young people beginning to read the New Testament should know
something of the argument and vision of the whole work. So in *From
Galilee to Rome* I give an abbreviated version of this book. When Luke
wrote it he included material from both *Mark* and 'Q'; since we have
already given these in the earlier parts, I now omit them and give his
own material only, which he probably set out in order before he came
upon *Mark.* In the later part of *The Acts of the Apostles*, I use only a
few representative stories about Paul ending with his famous sea-voyage

to Rome; saving the account of his ten years in the Aegean area and his trial in Palestine for the next part, *Paul the Explorer.*

For Paul, it seemed to me that, to begin with, what young people need is a sense of the kind of man he was and the sort of thing he wrote about—an introduction to him. I am always surprised by the hostility to Paul I find among young people; all they seem to think he did was to distort what Jesus had stood for and to suppress women in the Christian assemblies—so hard does mere gossip die. So I follow here John Knox's *Chapters in a Life of Paul* where he sets out a summary of Paul's own account of himself, and give an extended version of this (using Paul's autobiographical statement in Galatians as the scaffolding), so that the reader can listen to Paul's own words. I then give Luke's account of Paul's ten years in the Aegean area and his trial in Palestine.

In *Jesus—Leader and Lord*, I give selections from Paul to help the beginner to see what he thought important and how he went about explaining the Christian Faith: first what he had to say about Jesus, then a shortened version of *Romans* 1–8, and then selections to show what he had to say about the kind of questions young people raise—the difference Jesus has made and what he stood for, how the Christian life should be lived and how our Christian convictions are to be worked out in our actual day-to-day experience.

When I turned to the Fourth Gospel, I took the work of Dr. C.H. Dodd, *The Interpretation of the Fourth Gospel* and *Historical Tradition in the Fourth Gospel*, as my general guide. Here the principle I have been following all through—that young people have the right to share as far as possible the insight of great scholars, however simply this sort of sharing has to be done—is of especial importance, since so often this gospel is not dealt with in the classroom as the great original work it is. I owe my understanding of this gospel to the work of many scholars, but no works have so illuminated my understanding as Dr. Dodd's two books. So in setting out the argument and the dramatic pattern of the whole book and of its parts I have followed Dr. Dodd's suggestions. I think the notes I give in *New World* for young people themselves to read are a sufficient guide to what I have attempted to do.

This is how I read the Bible, and I hope that it helps the teacher and young people in the classroom and the uninstructed reader to see something of the story that makes the Bible the book it is. This, for me, is the heart of the Bible.

Beginning to read the Bible

We will begin with *Winding Quest.* We open it and begin to browse through its pages—which is what I would do with any book—to see what kind of book it is. We are aware very soon, from the way in which the pages are set out, that (perhaps to our surprise) both poetry and prose lie before us.

The habit of thinking of the Bible as, on the whole, a book of prose is so ingrained that we need to jog ourselves out of our controlling assumptions. The teacher should make sure that the young people he is teaching begin by enjoying this diversity of style and finding out what biblical prose and poetry—both with as much variety as English prose and poetry have—are really like, comparing it with what may be found in anthologies like *The Oxford Book of English Prose* or Helen Gardner's *The Faber Book of English Religious Verse.* We must get it quite clear that the Bible is to be read as a real book.

Winding Quest and *New World* are printed and arranged so that young people can pick them up, enjoy looking at them, browse through them and begin to read in them with pleasure. What stubborn mis-conceptions and attitudes we have to get rid of before we can really begin to read the Bible is illustrated by a girl's remarks about *New World*, 'It doesn't look like a Bible—it's too bright!'

In Appendix B I give a list of prose and poetry that a teacher might well go on to deal with so that young people can see what kind of book the Bible is.

The variety of the Bible

We now turn to look, in greater detail, at the variety of prose and poetry to be found in the Bible.

PROSE

One of the sources of the liveliness and freshness of the Bible is to be found in its great variety of literary form. Even in the much smaller world of the New Testament we have unexpected variety—poetry, historical account, letters, visionary writing, 'gospels' (a unique literary form), tracts, the Fourth Gospel (which, in form and spirit, shows more than an echo of Plato's *Dialogues*—it might be called *The Dialogues of Jesus* though it uses, of course, other traditions, too). The Old

Testament, drawn from a wider national literature most of which is now lost, has a much richer variety of literary form.

HISTORICAL WRITING

Three great histories lie behind the narrative parts of the Old Testament: 'The Priestly History' (older material edited and added to by the Jerusalem priesthood) sixth century B.C.E.; 'The History of the Israelites in their Homeland' ('The Deuteronomic History') sixth century B.C.E.; 'From David to Nehemiah and Ezra' (written by an unknown historian c. 400 B.C.E.).

The first is found in the first part of the Old Testament, 'The Torah' (the first five books of the Bible, 'The Pentateuch'); the second in *Joshua-Judges-Samuel-Kings* (this history may have had *Deuteronomy*— later included in the Torah—as its original 'Preface'); and the last is to be found in *Chronicles-Ezra-Nehemiah* (originally one scroll). [1] It has been impossible, within the self-imposed limits of *Winding Quest*, to do justice to these impressive histories. But I have tried to give something from them all—as much as possible from the first two. The Priestly History will be found in 'What Kind of World do we live in?' (307 ff.); 'What Sort of Persons ought we to be?' (319 ff.); and in 'Escape from Egypt' (93 ff.), where I have given much of the narrative but greatly abbreviated the legal codes. I have drawn on the second in 'In the Highlands' (118 ff.), *Brief Hour of Glory* and *The Death of Two Cities*. I have used two brief stories from *Chronicles*, where the historian is drawing, it seems, on old material (173 f.)—Nehemiah's Diary (192 ff.) and a brief extract from what is known as Ezra's Diary—though there is some doubt whether this was actually written by him (200 f.).

In the New Testament I give Luke's account of Christianity (*From Galilee to Rome*).

The historians to whom we owe these historical writings were not just recording the past events of their country's history. They were indeed concerned to tell a real story, using such information and sources as lay to their hands; but they were concerned with the religious significance of the people's story rather than their political and military fortunes. Hence their omission of any real account of David's Philistine

---

[1] The teacher should read Peter R. Ackroyd's *The Age of the Chronicles*; this book and age have been neglected because of the age's obscurity.

wars or his imperial triumphs, and of proper accounts of some of their greatest kings. This is as true of Luke as it is of the authors of 'The Court History' and of the larger histories. They were concerned with both history and theology.

Their use of sources, as we shall see, was part of their search according to their own lights, for the truth of what had happened; they quoted these at length, even when they contradicted the argument the historian was developing (see, for example, the two versions of the creation of the world—307 ff., 311 f.).

The fact that the historical accounts of the Old Testament come down to us in this way is a real gain. It saves us from ever thinking that we can know what happened in the past once and for all, just like that. The past, if it is to be understood, has to be constantly under reappraisal. Each generation has its own problems and its own questions; and it is in the light of these that it explores the past. That the Israelites, three times in their long story, were compelled to re-examine and remap their past, encourages us to be bold enough to ask our questions of it too. And we find another reassessment in the parables and poetry of Jesus and in the correspondence of Paul.

BIOGRAPHY AND AUTOBIOGRAPHY

The most outstanding examples of biographical writing are found in Baruch's 'Story of Jeremiah' (247 ff.) and Luke's account of Paul in the latter part of *The Acts of the Apostles* where he uses the story of Paul to crown his great argument and draws upon the diary (*N.W.* 190 ff., 190 ff., 235 ff.). But we have what amounts to biography in the picture of Saul and David (25 ff., 40 ff.) for what the writer has here to say about the religious convictions of his people is given through an account of their first two kings. And it is worthwhile noting that the accounts of the 'calls' of the prophets are often in the first person singular (Amos, 237; Jeremiah, 261 f.); and that we have a piece of Amos's disciples' account of their master—we wish they had thought it necessary to add more such biographical information ('Incident in the North', 232). There is much autobiographical material in Paul's letters; following a suggestion of John Knox, [1] I have gathered this material together in 'Paul's own Story' (*NW* 217).

[1] *Chapters in a Life of Paul*, pp. 49 ff.

PROPHETIC BOOKS

We find the prophetic poetry in four large 'rolls' of books—the Book of Isaiah, the Book of Jeremiah, the Book of Ezekiel and the Book of the Twelve.

The historians have included stories about some of the prophets in their histories; but these stories are either popular tales (like those about Elijah—224 ff.) or legendary (like those about Elisha, which I have not had space enough to use) or about Isaiah (175 ff.).

Our main information about the prophets, as far as we have any, is found in the four prophetic books. These were made and used by the prophets' disciples, and the books in which a prophet's original words were written down was expanded, added to and edited over the course of the years. They grew like this because they were living books used in worship and witness; the disciples were carrying on their founder's work and either commented on his sayings to show how important they were for later generations or added poems of their own. Sometimes they tell us very little about their founder (cf. Amos, 232 f.); sometimes they include a much fuller account as Baruch did in his 'Life of Jeremiah' (247 ff.).

The books about the prophets contain both poetry and prose. It is in the poetry that we find the original words of the prophet himself whose name the book carries; the prose is either biographical or auto-biographical.

I have not tried to give the reader a picture of any of the four great prophetic rolls. I have given selections from three of them (nothing from the Book of Ezekiel): Amos's poetry is found in the Book of the Twelve; the prophet of the Exile's poetry comes from the Book of Isaiah; I have given a fairly wide selection from the Book of Jeremiah. In these selections I have tried to help ordinary readers and young people to listen to the prophets themselves and to begin to understand why they took the stand they did. Hence, in addition to the actual poetry of the prophet, I have given also the biographical prose accounts where available (as for Jeremiah, 247 ff.) and Amos's and Jeremiah's accounts of their call (233 f. and 261 f.).

GOSPELS

These are not biographies but are a unique kind of literature which grew out of the living experience of the early Christian churches and are intended to set forth their faith; and it was part of their faith that what lay at the heart of their 'good news' had actually happened in Palestine 'under Pontius Pilate' not many decades before. They were not inventing a story to support their faith; their faith had sprung out of what had happened.

Stories about Jesus—what he did and what he said—first circulated as isolated units. The exception was the Passion Narrative which was recited in their worship from the earliest times. What we have in the gospels, therefore, is really the Passion Narrative (which occupies nearly a third of the story) and an introductory account of who it was who was brought to such a death. When men like Mark and Luke came to make their different accounts, they had at their disposal many varied collections of stories and sayings as well as eyewitness accounts.

I have explained what I believe about the nature of the stories and sayings in the brief notes for young people in *New World*, and also in the article dealing with the mission of Jesus in *A Source Book of the Bible for Teachers* (pp. 264 ff.); and I would commend to the teacher Dr. C.H. Dodd's *The Founder of Christianity* (pp. 17 ff.) and Dr. C.F.D. Moule's *The Birth of the New Testament* (pp. 86 ff.) for further information.

LETTERS

The presence of letters in an authoritative statement of faith like the New Testament is a remarkable fact. The story of how Paul's correspondence came to achieve this status has puzzled scholars. It has been suggested that, after his death and because of the controversial stand he had taken on the Jewish question, his letters were cherished only in the churches to which he had sent them. About the end of the century, however, they were published in Ephesus (having been re-covered from the church chests in the different cities to which they had been sent), with *Ephesians*, possibly, as a preface. [1]

It seemed to me that, at a first reading, young people need to make Paul's acquaintance before they plunge into the letters themselves which, as another New Testament writer admits, 'contain some obscure passages.' [2] Hence, I give only one whole letter, the shortest, *Philemon*

[1] cf. C. Leslie Mitton, *The Formation of the Pauline Corpus*; John Knox, *Philemon among the Letters of Paul*.

[2] 2 Peter 3.16.

(*NW* 326). But I give long selections from the other letters to show the liveliness and insight with which he writes and to help the reader to see what he really had to say about Christian life and faith and about some of the moral questions of his time. Among these, I have given the heart of his statement of faith (*Romans* 1–8, *NW* 295 ff.) and his discussion of the centrality of love as the Christian way (1 *Corinthians*, 12–14 – *NW* 312 ff.). I am sure that this experience is necessary if young people are to go on to tackle the full letters. These are real letters the difficulties of which arise not only from the depth of their thought but from the first-century style of argument (cf the discussion of Abraham in Romans 4, *NW* 302 f.).

LEGAL WRITINGS

Legal writings are never easy to read; where, as in the Bible, different codes have grown into one another, it needs the knowledge of an expert to sort things out. But some acquaintance is necessary, if readers and young people are to be encouraged to face the fact that religious convictions are more than individual matters and need to be embodied in the life of society. This is a slow and demanding process. In the Old Testament, we can see how the growing insight of the best men and women slowly changed the structure and the legal system of Israelite society. Some of the codes were working codes like 'The Ten Words' (108 ff.); some (like *Deuteronomy*), while based on older codes, were sketches for a future that never came. All this shows how men came to believe that religion is not merely an individual matter, and that social practice must be made to fit more nearly to their deepening convictions about God and man.

In the New Testament, we can see the need for rule and order, a new 'Torah', emerging. Paul at the end of his letters turns to moral problems and seems to quote collections of moral teaching which were beginning to be drawn up and used in the Christian communities for the guidance of their members and in missionary work; I include some of his discussions in 'How to go about it' (*NW* 321) and 'Tackling the Job' (*NW* 326 ff.) where he is probably using some of these collected rules; for example, *Romans* 13, 8–10 (*NW* 325) is probably such a piece of Christian teaching, quoted by Paul to reinforce his own exposition of Christian love. [1]

[1] cf E.G. Selwyn, *The First Epistle of Peter*, p. 414.

People who take religion seriously—and especially Christians—in every society have to face this issue; how difficult and contentious it can be is clearly seen by the way in which decisions of the British Council of Churches on international affairs have been received. This aspect of religious obligation needs to be discussed with young people; I have included the legal material both for its own sake and as a 'jumping-off ground' for discussion.

CREATIVE WRITING

This is the only term I can think of to describe literature in the Bible which is often mishandled and misunderstood. It is writing whose sources may be most varied—tribal tradition (as in *Genesis*, *Exodus*, *Judges*); popular stories such as lie behind *Jonah* and *Ruth* and the story of Joseph in *Genesis*; folktales such as that used in *Job*; 'myth' (a widely misunderstood word, but a technical term we cannot evade— see *Winding Quest*, 305) as in the first eleven chapters of *Genesis*. Here we have material that is often read as though it were plain history.

It is important to realize what these different types of material are; but it is more important to realize what the writers have done with them and what they are saying through them. The parables of Jesus have the same varied sources; memories from his boyhood, incidents in national life, popular stories circulating among the villages, local experiences—all transformed by the mind of Jesus and made to serve as the vehicle of his vision.

Here are three examples.

Genesis is part of a wider work, but it illustrates vividly what a writer (or writers) can do with different kinds of material—'myths', tribal traditions, popular stories.

'Myths' are stories which early people use to express their convictions about what we would call 'ultimate questions'—why there is a world at all? what and who is man? what is the meaning of human history? why is there evil?—'the great educative myths', as C. Day Lewis calls them, 'which from earliest times inch by inch enticed man forward out of his brutishness'. [1] In these stories they embodied what they thought about the world (what we should call their 'science' and their 'history'); but the important things about them is not their 'science'

---

[1] *The Poetic Image*, p. 32.

and their 'history' but their convictions of what makes life worthwhile
and whether the world has any meaning or not. The Israelites shared in
the common knowledge and 'myths' of the Middle East. We have
recovered versions of the stories they used which were circulating in
other parts of the then known world—in the Tigris and Euphrates
valleys, for example, and in the old town of Ugarit on the north
Palestinian coast. But, among the Israelites, the stories have been transformed and made to be the vehicle of their new vision of God and the
world and man which they owed in the first place to Moses. The writer
of *Genesis* used them as the opening phase of his story—they were to
be the preface to the story of his people who, he believed, had been
called to be in some sense (to use the words of a much later prophet) the
'servant' of God and of the world. I have set them out so that their
purpose can be clearly seen in 'What Kind of World do we live in?' (307)
and I have called attention in my comments to the way in which, if we
wish to discuss these 'ultimate questions', we need to use a story to
convey our meaning (305).

In the same way he uses the tribal traditions which lie behind the
stories of Abraham and Jacob and the popular story which lies behind
the story of Joseph (319 ff.). These are interesting to explore; they
disclose, as we now know, real information about the past tribal experience. But this is, again, not the important thing; the important thing is
the creative vision which the writer's use of the stories sustains. In
Genesis he is 're-mapping the world' and giving a vision of God as Lord
of history and of mankind as called to be his people.

Daniel, too is a much misunderstood book. It consists of stories and
visions, and it comes, so scholars believe, from the days of the Maccabean
Rebellion (168 B.C.E.). The stories had probably long been popular
stories circulating in the third century to sustain the people's resistance
to persecution and oppression and to the temptation to abandon their
faith. This need was urgent when Antiochus Epiphanes tried to ex-
tinguish both Jewish culture and Jewish religion. The writer of *Daniel*
seized on the idea of using these stories to strengthen the resistance and
encourage the loyalty of his people (though he had doubts about the
Rebellion itself), and he made them the preface to his visions in which
he saw the whole stage of history, the rise and fall of nations and the
triumph, against all odds, of his own people. This kind of literature needs

to be seen against the 'underground literature' of twentieth-century small peoples who have resisted the attempt to corrupt and destroy their own way of life (371 ff.).

In the New Testament we meet the same kind of imaginative litera-ture which again is often misunderstood—the parables of Jesus (which have been turned into little moral or theological tales) and the Fourth Gospel (which has been mixed up with the synoptics, as many Agreed Syllabuses show). I have said enough in *New World* itself (school edition only for the parables of Jesus; for the Fourth Gospel *NW* 344–350), to make merely a reference to them here sufficient. The point to note is that we are dealing in both the parables of Jesus and the Fourth Gospel with imaginative literature of the highest kind. The Fourth Gospel differs from the so-called 'synoptic gospels' not so much in its purpose (all are religious books setting out the Christian Faith) but in the range and scope and originality of its method, structure and argument (see especially 'The Book of Signs', *NW* 355–359).

I need only add a reference to the folktale from which the author of *Job* lets his poetry soar—a spring board from which to reach the central question which he thought even the great prophets were in danger of taking too much for granted: 'Can we really know anything at all about God?'

POETRY

One of my special concerns in making *New World* and *Winding Quest* is to open the whole world of biblical poetry to young people. They think the Bible 'boring' and 'dull', they say. But if ever there were living words, able still to move those who hear them, here they are—from the many-coloured poetry of *Job* and the passionate poetry of the prophets to the quiet and measured lines of the Twenty-third Psalm or the deceptively simple poetry of Jesus.

The historians have their own indispensable role to play in bringing home to us what I would call the 'vision' which sustains the whole of the Bible; the central and most memorable insights are to be found in the poetry.

The first thing for young people to do is, as I have said, to open *Winding Quest* and *New World* (or a modern translation of the Bible where poetry is printed as poetry) and just browse, getting the feel of

the poetry, noting its varied imagery and the way it can climb to the
heights or sink to the depths of mood and theme: national hymn and
tribal song, dramatic poetry, meditative verse, public satire and passionate personal utterance. And then—to go on browsing, letting the poetry
have its own way.

We have become so habituated to reading the Bible as a sort of
textbook on morality and theology that we need to shake ourselves
free of the habit and learn to read it in a relaxed and open frame of mind.
We need to cultivate the habit of listening.

Poetry needs to be listened to. And so it should be read aloud. Most
of the Bible was spoken prose and poetry. Men and women heard it
recited. The great stories were recited in worship in shrine and temple.
The prophets addressed people directly on the street or in the temple
court. Jesus's parables were first heard on village threshing floors and
his poetry spoken to friends or enquirers. Paul's letters were read aloud
in Christian assemblies, and the Fourth Gospel was probably first heard,
as Dr. W.F. Howard used to say, as sermons in Christian worship. The
poetry is certainly direct and spoken poetry—'Listen!'

This is important. There is a close affinity between poetry—indeed,
between all art—and religion. The poet is not so much concerned to
explain things as to help the listener or reader to share his experience and
to see the world (so he believes) as it really is. He wants us to look. He
is concerned with the way we feel as well as the way we think. Hence
he uses the devices of rhythm and rhyme and the evocative power of
words to enable us to stand where he stands and see with his eyes. It is
this power of poetry to move us—to make us aware, through words and
images and pictures drawn from the world we know, of a world that we
do not yet know—that links it with religion and makes it the most
effective vehicle for expressing religious insight.

It may be as well if we pause here to note, very briefly, the difference
between prose and poetry. Let us first set down a piece of prose and two
brief poems from the Bible, each dealing with God's care and love; and
then put alongside them what a modern literary critic has to say about
prose and poetry.[1]

---

[1] Compare, too the prose and poetry given on pp.23 ff.

Here is Paul (*NW* 293):

You see what it all comes to: our simple trust in God our Father puts us right, and we've nothing to worry about. This is what Jesus made possible. He made God's love real to us; and we are happy people, because we know that we can learn to be like God himself (we were created 'in his image') and live in his Way.

We can now be happy even when we have to face hard times. We know that hard times train us never to give in; never giving in is the secret of growing up; and being grown-up (as Jesus was grown-up), we look forward with high hope to the future. We aren't dreaming; for God himself lives in us, and our hearts are full to overflowing with his love.

Now one of Jesus's poems (*NW* 98):

> Keep asking—it will be given you;
>   keep looking—you will find;
>   keep knocking—the door will be opened.
> Everyone who keeps asking, gets;
>   everyone who keeps looking, finds;
>   to everyone who keeps knocking, the door opens.
>
> What father will give a stone to his boy
>   if he asks for bread?
> What father will give him a snake
>   if he asks for fish?
> Fathers are not all they should be,
>   but they know how to give the very best to their children.
> God is far better than our fathers;
>   of course he will give the very best to those who ask him.

Here is a poem on the same theme written over six hundred years before Jesus lived (289):

> Why do you talk and grumble,
>   you who are my people?
> 'God can't see what's happening to us,
>   'he isn't bothered about us and our rights!'
>
> Don't you know?
>   haven't you heard.
> GOD is always God,
>   creator of the whole universe!
>
> He does not faint or fail,
>   he knows what we can never know.
> He gives new life
>   to those who are worn out;
> He revives
>   those who are ready to drop!

Commandos get tired and faint,
    seasoned veterans fall out with fatigue;
but those who trust GOD
    grow stronger and stronger—
        soaring like eagles,
        running without tiring,
        marching without flagging!

Now think about these words of E.W.F. Toulmin:

It is a commonplace that the behaviour of language in prose is different from
its behaviour in verse; what the difference is may not be so clear. As with many
distinctions so fine as to resist precise formulation, an example may instantly
illuminate it. The lines are from Yeat's *The Crazed Moon*:

Crazed through much child-bearing
The moon is staggering in the sky.

The image, a brilliant one, is to be seized in itself. The thought behind the
image enjoys no independent existence, affords no additional satisfaction. Concept
and intuition are one, but only in the sense that the distinction has not yet arisen.
The language of prose, though not without its inner quality, enjoys at the same
time a kind of external existence; it lives for something beyond itself, namely the
communication of a meaning or idea. It is a means to an end. In prose we first
become aware of the distinction between what is said and what is meant. Hence
some of the repetitiveness of prose, and the still greater repetitiveness of
conversation. [1]

Now look back on the three quotations I have given, and consider if
the poems of Jesus and the Prophet of the Exile are not dealing with the
theme of God's love in a way quite different from that of Paul in the
quotation from his great argument in *Romans*.

Winding Quest and *New World* have been made and arranged to give
this poetry the importance it deserves. Here is a note about the theory
of Hebrew poetry and what I have done about it.

The principle of Hebrew poetry is the principle of what has been
called 'parallelism'. [2] It was rediscovered in the eighteenth century by
Robert Lowth, Professor of Poetry at Oxford. This is how Professor
Murray Roston describes Robert Lowth's rediscovery:

'The first pointer to the new theory he found in the frequent references to
antiphonal singing, which was probably an ancient tradition before the books of

---

[1] Pelican Guide to English Literature: *The Modern Age*, p. 321.
[2] For a full description of this see T.H. Robinson, *The Poetry of the Old
Testament*.

the Bible were written. Miriam, taking a timbrel on the shores of the Red Sea, *answered* Moses in words similar in sense and rhythm to his own; and when David returned from slaughtering the Philistines, the women ". . . *answered* one another as they played and said, Saul hath slain his thousands, and David his ten thousands". This last verse suggests two groups of women singers, one of which sang the first half of the verse *Saul hath slain his thousands* while the second responded with *and David his ten thousands.* Whether or not this particular passage was rendered antiphonally is immaterial. It is clear, however, that an early antiphonal tradition had moulded the form of Hebrew poetry not merely by dividing the line into two halves, but by ensuring that the second section should echo (by corroboration or contrast) the meaning of the first. The effect of such parallelism is to establish in Hebrew poetry a rhythmic ebb and flow, a sense which doubles back upon itself, rather than the linear forward movement of classical verse. But even more important, it employs instead of the rigid metrical laws of Greece and Rome a loose structural relationship of phrases, parisonic only in so far as each verse could be sung to the same tune.' [1]

This device of parallelism is capable of infinite variety in the hands of a great poet; both prophet and poet show its immense power to explore the heights and depths of human emotion.

Jesus used this same device as was made plain by C.F. Burney in his book *The Poetry of our Lord* which was published in 1925. Jesus's poetry, moreover, shows a widening of the range of parallelism; [2] he matches not only clause with clause but strophe with strophe, deepening its dramatic power (see *NW* 100, 102, 111, 113).

Here are some forms of biblical poetry.

Traditional poetry: the Ballad of the Kishon River (123) and the old song on p. 107.

Popular poetry: the girls' song on p. 40 and the 'strike song' on p.194. Village songs probably lie behind the songs in 'The Loveliest Song' (382). Such songs also lie behind some of the prophetic poems; the prophets used their rhythms and even their very words to strike home to the imagination of their hearers.

Scholars' poetry ('Wisdom' poetry): A Scholar's Poem (357); *Job* (361 ff.); 'Nothing's worthwhile!' (379); 'The Word of God' (*NW* 351 ff.) (where echoes of the opening words of *Genesis* mark the opening stanza). A very old poem may lie behind that account of creation itself (some scholars have thought that as we have it now it is in poetic form; it is for these reasons I have printed it as verse.)

---

[1] *Prophet and Poet*, p.22.

[2] See T.W. Manson, *The Teaching of Jesus*, p.54.

The Psalms. Recent research has brought the Book of *Psalms* to life by showing how varied are the types of literary form to be found within it. Its setting is the worship of the temple, and, although there are later psalms in it, most of the psalms reflect the religious life of the Israelite people before the disaster of 586 when the worship of the temple was almost brought to an end. Professor G.W. Anderson lists the types of psalms as follows: simple hymns like Psalm 100 (396), Psalm 148 (398) and Psalm 29 (386); communal laments like Psalm 44 (398) and Psalm 29 (209); royal psalms like Psalm 2 (206) and Psalm 74 (206); individual laments like Psalm 51 (402); individual songs of thanksgiving like Psalm 66 (215). Other forms have been suggested: wisdom poems like Psalm 73 (406); communal songs of thanksgiving like Psalm 65 (309); and Temple liturgies like Psalm 46 (394). I have tried to indicate the variety of form in the way I have arranged and described the psalms I have chosen (See Appendix A).

There are traces of early Christian hymns in the New Testament. I give what is perhaps the most well-known example (*NW* 293).

I have handled the poetry of the Bible in this way.

With the poetry of Jesus, where we are dealing with brief poems and only a small collection (35 in all), I did no more than let a simple, straightforward translation carry the rhythm. With the longer poems and the larger collections in the Old Testament I felt that such a procedure did not help the reader to feel the real impact of the poetry and indeed gave it, for English ears, a slightly artificial sound.

What I did was to try to see the poem or hymn as a whole, and, while keeping as far as possible to its structure and using its words, to catch something of the feel of an English poem. I soaked myself in the poetry, and, with its words and imagery sounding in my ears, put down the substance of what the poem was saying, sometimes using parallelism and sometimes alliteration to achieve this. I then went over the original poem and my own version to see that nothing vital was missed or distorted, and compared what I had done with the New English Bible and the Jerusalem Bible versions. What I was seeking here was not a full version, but enough to show young people that it was real poetry dealing with real themes and worth reading for its own sake.

The presence of poetry in the Bible, moreover, enables the teacher to deal with a deeper need of young people. I would agree with Harvey

Cox that the difficulty many young people and their elders find where religion is concerned

'is not merely an intellectual one. It is also intuitive and aesthetic. Men today do not simply complain that they cannot believe in God on intellectual grounds. Indeed a religious explanation of the universe may be just as conceptually adequate as another one. That is not the problem. The problem is that people do not "experience" or "encounter" God. Religious language including the word "God" will make sense again only when the lost experiences to which such words point become a felt part of human reality. If God returns we may have to meet him first in the dance before we can define him in the doctrine.' [1]

Here, in the Bible, where language is not the austere language of intellectual debate, but the intuitive language of awe and joy—where the remembrance of a skyline, a sudden east wind or a cry from the Jordan Valley can become the living imagery by which the meaning of human history can be grasped, a man's experience of the mystery of the world can be given form and his sense of the presence of God be communicated to others—the poet's awareness is everything. And the awareness is brought home to us with an abrupt directness of speech and a sharp, down-to-earth imagery that can still speak to the heart and 'stab us wide awake'. May not this be the first step for young people to the 'lost experiences' of which Harvey Cox spoke and the recognition that religious language makes sense? If so, young people can say Yes or No to the convictions that are being expressed for the right reasons, and not, as so often seems to happen, for the wrong ones.

MANY SOURCES

Scholars have thrown a great light on the making of the Bible, and it is important for the teacher to use this knowledge in the classroom, not as interesting information but as something that needs to be known if the Bible is to be properly read. It was made as real books are made, and this should be made clear, in however simple a way, from the very beginning.

Scholars have shown that historians and editors used many sources in making the books that now lie before us. The historians used many traditions, written and oral, in the making of their histories; the editors of the prophetic 'rolls' used previous collections of poems and made

[1] *The Feast of Fools*, p.28.

their own arrangements of them; the writers of the gospels used collections of stories about Jesus and of his sayings as well as the Passion
Narrative accepted in the churches where they wrote. The editor who
gathered together the letters of Paul for publication had previous
arrangements of some of his letters. I have arranged *Winding Quest* and
New World so that a teacher can explore these sources, in a simple way,
with his pupils. I have tried to give, within the limits of my purpose, a
little idea of what these sources were like. [1]

With the Pentateuch, I have followed the earliest sources 'J' as my
main source; but I have used 'E' material as well (see Appendix B).
Young people can compare the two and see something of their different
point of view. 'E' is especially important in its account of Moses's
'Mountain Experience' (95).

In *Brief Hour of Glory* I have followed the early source of *Samuel*
which included 'The Story of the Ark', popular stories about Saul and
David, and 'The Court History'. In *The Death of Two Cities* I give
selections from what seems to have been a 'History of Solomon'; then
the stories about the various reigns which come from Northern and
Southern Court Archives or from accounts which come from prophetic
circles (e.g., the stories about Elijah and Micaiah). I have omitted the
editorial comments.

In the New Testament, I have set out the story of the ministry of
Jesus from *Mark* in *The Beginning* and the teaching of Jesus in *The
Message* so that the individual stories, which Form-History research has
recovered, are sufficiently clear for the teacher to use them in a simple
way in the classroom when he is dealing with the making of the gospels.
The substance of *The Message* is the material usually referred to as 'Q'.

In *From Galilee to Rome*, I have given, in Part One, the special
material of Luke's gospel, referred to as 'L' (his final edition of his
gospel included material from *Mark* and 'Q' as well). In Part Two, I
have indicated the passages from the Diary, as I have also done in the
passages from *The Acts of the Apostles* in *Paul the Explorer*.

In the version of the Fourth Gospel in *Jesus—Leader and Lord*, I
have followed Dr. C.H. Dodd's suggestions in his *Historical Tradition
in the Fourth Gospel*; and I indicate material he believes may have come

[1] See pp.39 f. where I show how I have used these sources to abbreviate and
simplify the biblical material.

from the Ephesian tradition of the ministry of Jesus (the counterpart of Mark's Gospel in Rome) by describing it as 'narratives' at the beginning of each 'Sign'.

Here are some minor sources:

Army lists (58); government archives (146 ff.); temple records (151); legal documents (108; 184 ff.); tribal stories (130 ff.); diaries (251; *NW* 205, 242, 262 ff.); popular stories about Saul (25 ff.); the Elijah stories (224 ff.). For popular stories about Jesus, see Appendix C.

Insights and convictions

The Bible records a real and moving story; the very variety of literary form we encounter deepens the immediacy of its passion and pity. As we read, we begin to realize that certain great names dominate the story—Moses, David, Amos, Jeremiah, Isaiah, Jesus, Paul and John. They dominate the story because their profound insights opened men's minds and affected their lives. Without them the kind of story the Bible records would never have been written.

There is a sense in which we might think of the whole Bible as setting out the insights and convictions of these outstanding minds. The historical narratives of both the Old and New Testaments have been written under their inspiration; this is true of both the great histories of the Old Testament and of the gospels and *The Acts of the Apostles* in the New Testament. So we can read these historical narratives, not only for what they tell us about the events they are describing (what happened to the Israelite people, what Jesus said and did), but also for what they tell us about the convictions and beliefs of the men who wrote them. The historians are doing more than record past events; they are surveying what has happened in the light of the insights of the prophets (in the Old Testament) or in the light of Christian experience (in the New Testament). In the first three parts of *Winding Quest* and *New World* I have set out these historical narratives so that they can be read straight through and the underlying convictions of the historians and evangelists be noted. The whole arrangement of *Winding Quest* and *New World* is intended to encourage young people to read widely and at length in the biblical story and so get the feel both of the course of events and of what men believed these events had taught them—what, in a word, were the convictions that impelled them to write the story down.

To help young people to come as far as possible into direct touch with these great minds, I arranged their remembered sayings according to their literary form. Here I followed the work of biblical scholars; this explains the actual form of the sayings I have given (see, for example, Amos's poem 'You did not come back to me!'—240; Jeremiah's 'Confessions',—262 f.; Jesus's poem 'God's way must be our way'—*NW* 124; and compare these with the version in the Revised Standard Version of the Bible).

In dealing with these insights and convictions, it is important that young people should realize that they did not come 'out of the blue'. I have described the sources of the insight of the prophets in *Winding Quest* pp. 222 f., and I need not repeat what I have said there. I would only add that all this is as true of the parables and poetry of Jesus as of the poetry of the prophets. There is a deceptive simplicity about his words: behind them lie (a) an accurate observation of human behaviour, (b) a profound understanding of his people's history as he read it in 'the law and the prophets' and (c) his own awareness of God as 'Abba' ('Father'). He was not 'just moralizing'.

Further, since these insights and convictions are expressed in poetic form, it is essential not to dismiss the imagery as unimportant.

The imagery poets use comes from the depths of their experience. For example, the imagery of Jesus (if we are to be guided by what poets tell us about themselves) lay far back in his boyhood experience and had grown in his mind to match and express his deepest convictions and insights; he thought in stories long before he used them to communicate his insights to others. They were the original sources of his own insights rather than adduced or employed to confirm insights independently arrived at. [1]

Let us pause for a moment to look more closely at the imagery of biblical poetry. I have given in the school edition of *The Message* (pp. 15 ff.) a simplified version of Dr. C.H. Dodd's picture of the small-town world of Galilee as it is to be seen in the imagery of Jesus. [2]

Let us explore the imagery of Amos's poetry in the same way and look at his world through his eyes. I use only the imagery found in his poetry.

[1] H.J. Cadbury, *Jesus: What Manner of Man*, p.53.
[2] *The Authority of the Bible*, pp. 148 ff.

His world was the world of the countryside and the villages—tending fruit trees, oxen ploughing, men treading the threshing-floor, sheep farming, bird-trap and gin, houses being built, cows being turned into the byre, the last fruit being carried back from the harvest field; a world with its familiar sights: high cedar and sturdy oak, the harvest cart rocking on the bumpy village road, a bird dropping suddenly from the sky, a charred stick in the winter fire. But it was all set against the tragic backcloth of border warfare—burning houses and raped women—and unpredictable natural disaster—whirlwind, drought, forest fire, locust, wild beast of the forested hills or the Jordan Jungle. There was danger on the roads; people travelled in company—you never knew what you might meet, bandit or lion or bear, and even roadside huts had their snakes. A trumpet would suddenly be blown in a village and village gates shut—bedouin raiders had been seen in the hills. The distant roar of a lion—common sound on a still night—or the frightening growl in a near-by thicket symbolise the persistent danger in which men lived. A pair of knuckle-bones or the tip of an ear might be all that was left of a sheep. The narrow gorges—stony and dry in the summer, turbulent torrents in the winter—made a man dream of the reliable Nile and the rise and fall of its full waters. And over all was the majesty of darkness and light.

I call attention to the imagery of the prophets and of Jesus, in a chapter devoted to 'insights and convictions', because the imagery of poem or parable is not there just to illustrate some 'timeless' truth; it is there because that is the way poets think and feel and the only way in which they can make us aware of their convictions and insights. 'The image is the constant in all poetry,' says C. Day Lewis, 'and every poem is itself an image . . . Metaphor remains the life-principle of poetry, the poet's chief test and glory.' [1] To paraphrase a poem is to destroy it; to listen to a poem and to let its words and imagery fill our mind is the only way to enter the poet's world and to share his vision.

This is true of all prophetic poetry but it is supremely true of the parables and poetry of Jesus. 'Truth appeared in his mind, in the form in which he taught it. He is not borrowing illustrations or customary forms of presentation—all of his teaching has the air of fresh and vivid personal insight.' [2]

The parables and poems of Jesus can be read at different levels. They are short stories (like his 'Village Stories', *NW* 90 ff.) or pictures of life on a farm (like his stories of 'The Big Farm', *NW* 75 ff.) or a poem on eyesight (*NW* 104). The sting of story and poem is, as Dr. Alec Findlay

[1] *The Poetic Image*, p.17.
[2] W.W. Fenn, *The Theological Method of Jesus*, quoted by H.J. Cadbury in *Jesus: What Manner of Man?* p.86.

used to say, 'in the tail'. But there is more. Here, in the selction of
incident and the economy of word (which shine through his friends'
memories of what he said), we have not only, to use C. Day Lewis's
words, 'the perceptive eye' but also the 'interpreting imagination'. And
here, in hints of Old Testament imagery (even, occasionally, actual
quotations: see 'Where the Wild Birds roost' and 'Out with the Sickle!'—
NW 70, 82; and the story in which he begins by quoting Isaiah—NW 40 f.)
he is dealing with the whole significance of the history of his people and
God's work for the whole world through them. He is calling everybody
everywhere to share that vision of God and Man which he had and to
look with his eyes at the world as they know it in their own experience.

I have set out my selection from Paul's letters and my version of the
Fourth Gospel with the same end in view; here the reader can see how
our whole Christian experience compels us to re-examine all our convictions and to see the whole of human experience and history in a new
light.

In these days, when all convictions are being re-examined and all
affirmations subject to question, it is important to help young people
to see *how* convictions are come by and the way they arise out of living
situations. The Bible is not simply a record of the convictions and
insights men attained; it is the record, too, of how they were made.

Debate and clue

These convictions and insights, now set down in the disciples' reports
of their teachers, are not the insights of isolated individuals; they are
part of a whole people's story. This is the third stage to move on to; and
I have set out *Winding Quest* and *New World* so that this can be seen.

The first three parts of *Winding Quest* describe, in their own words,
the way in which the Israelites held on to two convictions: that the
God they worshipped—who had led them out of Egypt, made a
Covenant with them and led them to their new homeland—was alone
Lord of history and nature; and that the world they found themselves
in, despite its tragedies and disasters, its strange and terrible imperfections
and evil, was his world. They ultimately rejected the polytheism of their
neighbours (a commonsense solution of an imperfect world) and held
doggedly on to what must have seemed even to themselves sometimes a
vast contradiction between their experience and their faith. This can

be seen in the history they chose to record and the way they recorded that history. The final disaster was the destruction of their political independence and the fall of Jerusalem itself. This climax is the core of their story: how can God be Lord of history and nature when this is the end of the homeland he gave them? Hadn't their conviction that they were 'God's People' been blatant self-delusion? Did religion matter after all?

This is what the prophetic and 'wisdom' poetry is about. This is, as I have said, the 'Great Debate'. It is in the relationship of the last two parts of *Winding Quest* to the first three parts that I have tried to help the reader to see what the debate was about (see 221 ff.).

New World is dominated by 'one man', Jesus. Here again I set out, in their own words, the account his friends gave of him and what Luke tells us of the spread of Christian communities over the known world. The last two parts show how the friends of Jesus tried to understand the meaning of his whole witness. They believed that the story of the Jewish people, and indeed the story of the whole world, came to a climax in the story of Jesus: here can be seen 'a purpose God planned and settled before history began' (*NW* 306). We can see how the debate of the Old Testament (often quoted) is believed by the friends of Jesus to reach its answer in him. The debate is still going on; but here are men who believe they have been given the clue. In the relationship of the last two parts of *New World* to the first three parts I have tried to help the reader to see how early Christians came to their characteristic convictions (see especially 'Paul's own Story'–*NW*. 218 ff.; 'The Story of Jesus is Part of a much bigger Story'–*NW*. 295 ff.; and my notes on the Fourth Gospel–*NW*. 342 ff., 355 ff.).

Foundation documents

The Bible contains the 'foundation documents' of both the Jewish and the Christian communities. The fact that it is still read in worship shows that the Old Testament for Jews and the whole Bible for Christians have a theological as well as an historical significance for those communities.

I have already described the theme of both Testaments as 'steadfast love' (*chesed*) and 'love' (*agape*). These are not just timeless ideas or abstract conceptions. You will not find their meaning in a dictionary.

It is only by reading the story of the Israelite people that you will become aware of what 'steadfast love' means to them; it describes a known experience of them as a people. It is not an accident that when Paul is describing what 'love' means he gives a thumb-nail sketch of Jesus (*NW* 319) or speaks of the 'fellowship' experienced in the small Christian groups. Dr. Snaith calls attention to this when he translates *chesed* as 'Covenant love'. The love which is the theme of both Old and New Testaments is the love which was learned and known in the fellowship of a community—the Jewish 'people' and the Christian 'fellowship'. So it can be said that the theme of both Testaments is 'the People of God'. The love of which the Bible talks is a love which needs a community to express it and a world to express it in.

The making of the 'People of God' began with the 'Covenant' experience in the desert under the leadership of Moses. His work was to create out of very mixed tribal groups a 'people' who were to be the people of the God who had brought them out of Egypt. We might well describe the story of the whole Bible as an attempt to make this idea clear. It can be associated with various political groups, a tribal league (as with Moses) or a nation (as with David); it can be associated with a minority within a nation (as with the prophets) or even, as in the New Testament, with a 'fellowship' where all barriers between people have been broken down.

I begin *Winding Quest* with the Israelite people when they were the dominant nation in the area between the Euphrates and the Nile so that the reader shall know from the beginning that he is dealing with a real story about real people. Then I give *Memories of the Past* which is an account of their traditions, in their own words, of how they became, not a nation but a 'people' in a peculiar sense. What this word meant was to be the theme of the prophets and the concern of kings and common people; and their story is the story of the varied meanings this title, 'People of God', can carry. After the nation had been destroyed, we move on to the time when a prophet could think of the outcast Israelite people, homeless and powerless, as still, in a profound sense, the 'servant of God' and the 'servant' of the world. I have set out the prophetic poetry so that the reader can see what the prophets have to say about how 'God's People' should worship him and how they should live. This too is the theme of *Enduring Convictions* (see 309 f.) where

Abraham, Jacob, and Joseph symbolize the people; and the theme of *Jonah*, *Ruth* and *Job*. This is why the Israelites transformed the nature festivals of Palestine into celebrations of their spiritual journey as 'God's People'.

'The People of God' is taken up in the New Testament and is its consistent theme, from Jesus's call to his countrymen expressed in word and deed in *The Beginning* and *The Message* to the 'Table Talk in *Jesus—Leader and Lord*. I have tried to call attention to this in the way I have arranged the material—and the way I have translated, for example, the phrase 'Son of Man' which is a name for the People of God (*NW* 29), or set out Jesus's poems on 'How we can learn from what happened long ago' and 'The Doomed City' (*NW* 109 ff.).

'My history'

'It is only when ancient history can be seen as "my history",' writes Jaroslav Pelikan, 'does it spring to life, becoming a new and more fascinating mystery because of my involvement in it . . . What is sovereign over the past is likewise sovereign over my past.' [1]

This personal way of reading the Bible will take as many forms as there are readers; the Bible will 'find' people (to use Coleridge's famous words) in many different ways.

Winding Quest and *New World* have been planned to help young people to learn how to read the Bible at depth—not merely as ancient history or great literature or 'foundation documents', but as all these and something more.

I have never been able to keep my own reading of the Bible in different compartments, so to speak—reading it in one way when I am studying it and in another way when I am meditating on it. It is one book to me—a book I must read in the light of all I can learn about it from historian and scholar, but a book I can read at different levels. I do not forget that it is a particular book about particular people—this is its great strength for me. But as I go on reading, I become one of them until I feel I am beginning to look at the world I live in as they looked at theirs.

It is in the whole story that the Bible speaks to me, not just in its 'fine' passages. *Winding Quest* and *New World* are set out so that the

[1] *The Christian Intellectual*, p.76 f.

reader can survey the whole story and meditate upon it and see the passages that set profound insights to memorable words against their background of ordinary human experience. The Twenty-third Psalm or a parable of Jesus are not statements of timeless truth but insights into common life.

It is the sense of direction that matters and it is when the reader, having read the story and read it often, surveys the whole world of the Bible that he can see where the main roads are and what the sign-posts say.

WINDING QUEST *and* NEW WORLD *and the teacher*

When we are dealing with the Bible, we who are teachers may find ourselves, if we are not careful, dealing with everything except the Bible. Our present century has seen such as expansion of biblical research and discovery (especially where the Old Testament is concerned) and such a debate about the importance of the Bible that we may find ourselves swamped in their vast waters. The teacher who has had specialist training, knowing how much we owe to such research for our understanding of the Bible, may find himself giving far more time to these matters than to the actual text of the Bible itself. The teacher without specialist training, aware of the importance of all this research but little acquainted with it, may be so scared that he sticks in an almost literal manner to the specified passages of the Agreed Syllabus. *Winding Quest* and *New World* were planned to help both kinds of teacher.

I know myself, from my early experience of teaching, how easy it is for the teacher, dealing with so vast an area where he must somehow simplify his classroom material, to lose his sense of direction, be tempted too much by fascinating details or escape by sheer generalizations. I know how difficult it is, even with such helps as I have always made for myself as my marked Bible (where I indicate literary sources), or my 'scissors-and-paste' editions of either books or themes, to read the Bible as living literature. I early began typing out biblical material so that I could read it with joy. In making *Winding Quest* and *New World* I have used much of this working material of mine; they are the kind of books that I wish I could have had for my own reading and teaching.

They try to do two things: to help the teacher to catch a real glimpse of what I have called 'the sweep of the story', not in some abstract summary but in the living words of the writers themselves; and to help him to realize the creative significance of what, in the books of the scholars, are mere words or even letters on a page ('J' and 'P' and 'Q').

By 'sweep of the story' I mean more than the developing story; I mean also the developing argument, the growing convictions, the deepening insights. But these need to be discovered in the vividness of the actual literature itself; only so can we read it as we ought to read it 'till we can hear people talking' and be drawn into the 'unceasing conversation or debate'.

I have tried to help the teacher without specialist training not to be afraid of the mass of research and discussion he will find on the shelves of the libraries. Here he can see what light such scholarship throws on the biblical literature; I have given information about scholarly analysis or historical background(either by embodying it in the text or referring to it simply in notes and comments) sufficient for a first proper reading. *Winding Quest* and *New World* are intended to help such a teacher to begin to do just that, setting what he reads against its 'moment in time' (as Marc Bloch, the great French historian used constantly to insist) and yet sensing its immense relevance for our own time.

Because what I offer is the 'heart' of the Old and New Testaments, the teacher needs to widen his horizons to include much of the material that I have had to leave out or have not done justice to. There are the wider Old Testament histories to which I have referred that have much material I have had to omit, chiefly because *Winding Quest* is long enough as it is. There are the insights of other writers—the prophets I have not dealt with, the books of the New Testament I have omitted like *Hebrews* and *First Peter* and *James* and *Revelation*. Where Jesus is concerned, I have given a picture of him as his friends saw him through the material *Mark* used; the teacher needs to read the full gospels (especially *Matthew* to which I have done no justice at all) as living books themselves and to see how their writers were no mere compilers but genuine authors with their own vision and insights.

Finally, I have tried to help the teacher to become aware, not only of the 'sweep of the story', but also of what I would call 'the depth of the story'. The insights and convictions in the Bible, as I have said, grew out of 'lived history'. I have tried to help the teacher to see how this happened; he can then go on and test out what I have given with the full text of modern translations. I look upon *Winding Quest* and *New World* as simply the servants of these great modern achievements.

CHAPTER THREE

AT WORK IN THE CLASSROOM

Using *Winding Quest* and *New World*

With differing ages

I picked up my knowledge of the Bible as I grew up. I can hardly remember the time when I did not know it was there to read. I knew it was an adult book—that was part of its excitement for me: my father and mother themselves read it, my father read it aloud to us on Sunday morning (I always enjoyed this) and it was read and expounded in the adult services and meetings of the little chapel to which my family belonged. My father's library had big books in it that fascinated me. Among them were some large Bibles with drawings by famous artists—too large for me to hold; I had to pull them out on to the floor and lie looking at the pictures and reading here and there as my fancy took me. I can never remember my father ever saying to me about any book 'That's too difficult for you—wait till you're older'. I didn't understand much that I read, I am sure, but I knew I was reading an adult book, a book that mattered to my father—and that was fine.

I begin here because I have always coveted for the young people I have met an experience like mine—a natural approach to the Bible as an important book. Most of them had no such background of home and adult community where the Bible was taken seriously. Yet I am sure that the Bible is to be approached as a book to be explored and enjoyed however old you are.

But we must not confuse matters. We must begin with the Bible as the kind of book we know it is—a serious book about human history and human destiny. It is not a children's book. To have at its heart the death of two cities and the political execution of a young man is reminder enough of that. If we are not to trivialize the Bible, we must recognize it for what it is.

I think that it follows from this that such a book can only properly be studied with young people who have begun to ask the questions with which it deals. Because we have tried to teach too much too soon, we have produced in the minds of many young people serious misconceptions about the Bible. If they are to see what kind of book it is and to begin reading it in such a way that they will go on reading it after they have left school (because it is the kind of book that at school you can only begin to read), we need to see to it that it makes its main impact on them when they are of an age to realize what it is really about. Both *Winding Quest* and *New World* were made, in the first instance, for just such a time. The order in which I would think young people could best approach them would be *New World* first, and then *Winding Quest*. That is why there is a difference in set-up and print between the two volumes.

But before they come to the serious study of the Bible I think they should have been encouraged to find out that it is a book to be browsed in and enjoyed, a book of infinite variety and many colours. *Winding Quest* and *New World* were designed to be the kind of books that can be left about (at home and school) so that children and young people can do what I did—pick them up when they want to and read what they will. They cannot too soon get the 'feel' of the story in the Bible, its poetry and prose, its narratives and histories and letters—and so get a sense of its sweep. The pictures by Bernard Brett and Geoffrey Crabbe are part of this story—when I was planning the books I remembered what pictures did for me when I began to make the acquaintance of the Bible.

I think we have treated (and still treat) the Bible with improper dead-pan solemnity. I can remember being told when I was quite young, that the Bible was a book of God's commands (it was so read in the circles in which I grew up); and I can remember being puzzled by the question why a book of rules and laws should have so many stories in it and pictures—stories that sometimes didn't seem to keep the rules I was told were God's rules. But the Bible is much more than a book of rules. If its real theme is what I have suggested it is, then it is a book we can enjoy reading; and if we are to enjoy reading it, the sooner we learn to browse in it and explore it the better.

With younger children, I would think that two things are important: learning that there is a lot in the Bible exciting to listen to (if what the Bible is saying about God is right, then this is what we should expect); and beginning to explore the stories about Jesus and what Jesus himself had to say. That is why the first three parts of *New World* are written for a reading age of about 9 years (a listening age below that, of course); the rest of *New World* and all *Winding Quest* has a reading age of about 12 years.

The teacher of children must play this by ear. If he has read the two volumes so that the stories are running through his mind, he will know what is appropriate and when it is so. Top juniors can begin to explore the story in whatever way they and their teacher feel is what they want to do; and they can begin to learn how the Bible came to be the book it is. But all this should be so done that when they reach the secondary school they will be ready and eager for its more serious study. They will certainly know that it is not a fairy story—but that there are stories in it that begin (as we should put it) 'Once upon a time . . .' They will know something of the range of the Bible and the many different people they can meet in it. They will not be troubled by the wrong kind of 'contradiction' between 'What the Bible says . . .' and 'What other books in the school are saying'. But they will have begun to be aware that the Bible is more than stories about people—it is about the kind of world we live in, what God is like and how we ought to treat one another.

If it is kept in mind that in the primary school the teacher's business is to introduce children to the Bible and in the secondary school his business is to begin its serious study, a teacher should feel free to deal with the biblical material as and when he thinks fit. But in all this he must be discriminating, as he would be if he were dealing with any other comparable literature.

Let me give an example of the kind of discrimination I am thinking of. Take the stories in *Daniel* and the parables of Jesus. Because the stories in *Daniel* are popular stories—'The Fiery Furnace', 'The Lions' Den'—they may be thought just the sort of stories junior children like. The parables of Jesus, however, are not just the simple stories they seem—they carry deep theological insights; therefore 'the child's understanding of the parables is questionable'. [1] But is this so? We may think that there is reason for holding the Daniel stories back to a later age, when we remember that *Daniel* was a sort of broadsheet for guerrillas fighting in the hills, and that, if we separate the stories from the visions

[1] Quoted by Ronald Goldman, *Religious Thinking from Childhood to Adolescence*, p.6.

which follow them, we simply trivialize them. On the other hand, we remember that the parables of Jesus are the creations of a great poetic mind (see above, p.60) and can be understood at different levels. They are not allegories or illustrations of truth which can be stated in abstract terms; they are prose poems that, to be understood, must first be taken as real stories. If this is so, the fact that children cannot reproduce what *Matthew* (or somebody else) thought they meant is irrelevant; the important question is whether or not they can respond to the stories as stories. This seems quite a proper preparation for looking later at the same stories in a more profound way. It is when we moralize the parables and confine ourselves to only two or three (there are more than fifty to explore) that we destroy them. In the light of this kind of discrimination, a teacher might think that junior children can properly begin to enjoy the parables of Jesus as they can explore other great poetry or respond to great pictures and great music; but that he must approach them in the classroom in a way very different from the traditional way they have been dealt with there.

Winding Quest and *New World* have been planned for all ages to enjoy and explore as they are able. But I have had particularly in mind the needs of young people in secondary schools. I want them to enjoy the Bible and in their enjoyment to begin to study and understand what it is about—and not to turn their backs upon it as 'kids' stuff'.

How, then, should we approach the Bible in the classroom? Three ways matter: enjoying, exploring, understanding. You can't understand what you've not explored; and you can't explore, in any sense that is really significant, what you don't enjoy exploring. In a sense these are stages. And yet, in another sense, they belong together. If you enjoy something, you are always exploring it and finding new aspects of it; and as you enjoy and explore, you are beginning to understand. The kind of reading of the Bible I am concerned with is the reading that can go on for a lifetime, enjoying, exploring and understanding. *Winding Quest* and *New World* are intended to help young people to find out how richly rewarding such reading is.

Enjoying

Winding Quest and *New World* have been given the format they have so that they may be a joy to pick up and look at. With the Bible, this is

a most important first step. The idea of the Bible many young people
still have is that of a small book in black covers, with small print and
double columns to a page. It comes as a surprise to many that the Bible
can be printed like an ordinary book, with poetry printed as poetry and
conversations looking like conversations.

To make reading pleasurable, I have kept all references to chapters
and verses off the page and given what seemed to me to be natural titles
to story and poem, instead of the traditional or conventional titles,
which do not belong to the original text. I have let the narratives follow
their natural divisions, and the selections from Paul's letters and the
Fourth Gospel the natural stages of the argument. I have followed the
suggestions of reliable scholars in separating poem from poem. This is
only roughly approximate, of course; different scholars may have
different views of where a poem ends. But the important thing is that
young people should know that a chapter like *Isaiah* 40, for example,
is not one long poem but consists of several related poems (they could
discuss how I have divided the poems and whether they agree).

But reading, to be enjoyable, should be real reading. Much of the
confusion in readers' minds about the Bible comes from our habit of
reading it in bits—in passages too brief to give any sense of a developing
story. *Winding Quest* and *New World* have been set out so that whole
stories or series of stories can be read. The Bible should be enjoyed as a
book of complete stories before it can be effectively studied in detail.
Here are some 'wholes': The Court History (63 ff.); *Memories of the
Past*, where the picture of themselves that the Israelites brought with
them into Palestine can be seen; Baruch's 'Story of Jeremiah' (247);
the parables of Jesus as an anthology of stories (*NW* 67 ff.) where the
whole vision of Jesus can be seen (we miss this if we deal with parables
one by one—let parable interpret parable); the first part of Paul's letter
to the Roman Christians (Romans 1–8 – *NW* 295 ff.); the Fourth
Gospel as a piece of dramatic writing (*NW* 342 ff.).

But reading for themselves may not be the best way in which many
young people can begin to enjoy the Bible. They need to hear it read
aloud. This, as I have suggested, can be planned in many ways. *Winding
Quest* and *New World* have been made to be read aloud—when I was
making these versions, I read much of them aloud to various groups
to get the sound of them right.

Whether young people are fluent or slow readers, there are some parts of the Bible that ought, if possible, to be first heard read aloud.

The tribal traditions of *Genesis* and *Exodus* and *Judges* in *Memories of the Past* call for this treatment, for they were recited at the great festivals or told by story-tellers in the villages. If they are to be understood properly, something of this atmosphere needs to be created—they were never just pages in a history book. In their recital the tribes were remembering who they were by hearing again and again the traditional stories of their past.

The Passion Narrative, too, needs this approach, for it was first told in Christian worship, on the first day of the week.

Luke's stories of the early church and of Paul can be browsed through or read quietly. But the quotations of Paul's own letters call for reading aloud—which is how they were first heard in Christian assemblies.

All this seems important to me if the living quality of the Bible is to be brought out, and the idea that it is a dull book 'which just keeps ticking you off' is to be shown to be quite untrue.

The illustrations and the photographs have been planned to make enjoyment the first response. The photographs have been chosen to give a 'picture gallery' of the world of the Bible and, toward the end, of our own world. The paintings are not illustrations in the ordinary sense of the word—they are what the artists wanted to paint as their response to the story, and they say 'This is what we wanted to paint; what do you want to paint?' (or write or act or whatever).

Young people should be encouraged to respond creatively to what they have discovered. Practising teachers do not need anybody to tell them how this can be done; but many seem to feel that this is somehow inappropriate in religious education. The idea that religious education is 'moral instruction' or 'Bible teaching' dies hard, and the view of the Bible as a textbook haunts what we do. But such creative response is the true way of learning to enjoy the Bible.

'Things to Do' in the school edition of *New World* show how I think the New Testament should be explored.

Here are two suggestions for *Winding Quest* to help young people to widen their awareness of what they are reading. I have called attention to the 'living situations' which lie behind the Psalms and given some indication of what scholars think those situations were (202). When young people have read and discussed the narratives of *Brief Hour of Glory*, *Memories of the Past* and *The Death of Two Cities*, they could look through the psalms and see what situations recorded in the narrative they think may lie behind them (scholarly opinion now thinks that the Book of *Psalms* reflects, in the main, the religious situation before the Exile).

Young people again could be asked to look through the poems of the prophets, given in *Making Sense of the Story*, to note all the references to the escape from Egypt and the Covenant and to discuss what use the prophets made of this memory of the past.

The true joy of reading the Bible comes when we begin to realize that it is a real and living book. Unless this has been realized, all our attempts to make the Bible seen 'important' and 'relevant' will be either boring or self-defeating. A glance through what young people said about the Bible to Harold Loukes proves my point;[1] they had never learned to enjoy reading it.

Exploring

Explore—everything!

If the first approach the teacher should encourage in young people is to enjoy reading it and hearing it read aloud, the second is to encourage them to explore it in every way that seems relevant in the classroom situation.

We 'tell' our pupils too much: we prescribe what parts of the Bible they are going to read and we even point out to them what the passages they are reading mean. We rob them of the joy of finding out for themselves, and forget what we are helping them to read the Bible for. The result is that when they leave school they finish with the Bible too.

If young people have begun to enjoy the Bible, there ought to be no difficulty in discovering what they would like to explore in greater depth. The teacher will keep his ears open for significant comments or questions, and make these the points at which more serious exploration can begin.

I use the word 'exploration' for an important reason. The whole world of the Bible will take more than a lifetime to explore; in school, with the limitations within which the teacher must work, only a

---

[1] *Teenage Religion*, p.40.

fragment of that world can be explored. What matters is that the exploration should be begun—and begun at a point and in a direction that the young people think is worthwhile or that has captured their imagination; and the teacher, who has surveyed the whole landscape of the Bible and is himself still exploring it, should put his own knowledge of the landscape at their disposal. I think of exploring the Bible in much the same way, for example, as I know young people at schools, under the guidance of experienced teachers, explore Snowdonia. The strategy for leading young people in exploring Snowdonia is the strategy needed to explore the Bible.

I hope that *Winding Quest* and *New World* are such that they make the exploration of the Bible by young people an exciting as well as a manageable enterprise. They represent, at any rate, my explorations over many years; in a sense, they are my reports of the landscape of the Bible.

What should be explored must be settled by teacher and class together—it will depend on questions young people ask, the local situation out of which these questions arise and the teacher's judgment about the guidance these particular young people need.

The teacher should look through what I have said about the kind of book the Bible is and the way in which I have tried to set out its wealth of form and content, its underlying story and its emerging meaning in *Winding Quest* and *New World*. Something of all this young people have a right to know—but in their own way and to meet their own needs. The teacher must have surveyed the whole landscape (to keep the Snowdonia imagery) and found out the lie of the land; he can begin his class's exploration at the most accessible point.

It will be seen by now that I value this kind of personal and meaningful exploration as more important than 'teaching' the contents of the Bible at this stage. First-hand exploration of even a small part of the landscape is far better than being given second-hand information about a countryside you have never even seen.

I add a further note. The material in the Bible is told from various points of view; this should not be forgotten. It is not a final objective account of the whole events and situations it is dealing with; it has always this personal note. I have called attention to this in my comments; and I have given examples of it. I have given both the Israelite and the

Assyrian account of the siege of Jerusalem (175 f.); what might be called the prophetic and the lay account of Ahab—one hostile and one friendly (the Elijah stories—224 ff.; and 'The Last Battle'—161 f.); in *New World* young people can compare Mark's and Luke's accounts of Jesus. Exploration needs to be both critical and lively; there is more than one side to every story.

Understanding

If young people have begun to enjoy reading and exploring the Bible, they will have already taken their first steps to understanding the concern which sustains it and its meaning for us now.

The teacher cannot be too much aware of the real 'set' against any proper consideration of the Bible which is widespread today.

For example, Dan Jacobson, the author of two plays on Old Testament themes—*The Rape of Tamar* and *The Caves of Adullam*—has described the incredulity of his friends when it became known he was taking the Old Testament seriously. In an article about these plays, he quotes Evelyn Waugh's acid comment that an excessive interest in the Old Testament is often a sign of incipient insanity, and goes on to discuss why 'the Old Testament has a peculiarly bad reputation now-adays'. He thinks it is 'partly the result of Scripture teaching in schools which leaves everyone with a memory of some absurd stories, many outlandish names and a host of unseemly "begats".'

He may be right or wrong about that. What interested me is the way he came to take Old Testament stories seriously and began to understand something of what they were about. It began, he says, with fascination'.

What came first was a fascination with the story of the rape itself (see *Winding Quest*, 64 ff.) as a series of dramatic events, from the sickness of Ammon's desire for his sister to the revenge taken upon him years later by the doomed Absalom. The compression and completeness of the tale, its startling reversals of course, the truths about human nature hidden and revealed in the protagonists' terse words and violent actions: it was obviously impossible for me to think of the story in isolation either from the history that preceded it and followed it, or from my own relationship to that history.

He goes on to ask questions we have already asked; here, where we are thinking of young people's understanding of the Bible, they have an immediate relevance:

Where can we possibly belong, among those ancient, small wars, those codes of conduct that have become all but incomprehensible, those cosmographies which we know to be nonsensical? Where do the figures of the ancient world belong, among our aeroplanes, vast populations and relativities of judgment? Sometimes with varying admixtures of self-pity and self-admiration, we can't help feeling that we are absolutely marooned in our own time, it is so different from any that preceded it. But what is so strange about that feeling is that simultaneously we are likely to find ourselves overwhelmed by the knowledge of how close those apparently distant people of the past are to us, how short is the tether that ties us to them. Even the obscurity that surrounds so many of the heroes of antiquity can become, paradoxically, a mode of revelation: they emerge slowly into clarity, if we allow them to, rather as our own lives and motives can become visible to us. [1]

I have given these extracts at length because they are an account of how an adult, aware of all today's pressures and feelings, can come to take biblical writing seriously and begin to understand it. It may give us some guide to how young people, in their own way, may become aware of the Bible too. I note that Dan Jacobson uses the words 'explore' and 'revelation'. What began as a fascinating story became for him 'my history'.

In all understanding of the Bible it is necessary to distinguish between what I have called the 'vision' and the language and ideas with which the vision has been expressed. Insights can only be described in terms of the knowledge and conceptions of the time when they are seen. Young people who dismiss *Genesis*—because 'its science is ridiculous'— need to learn that we can only use the tools that lie to our hand; what we make with the tools is the important thing.

I would let young people look at a book like *The Explosion of Science* (edited by Sir Bernard Lovell and Tom Margerison and magnificently illustrated). Its sense of wonder and awe marks even the photographs that dominate the pages. Here is a vision of the physical universe as modern scientists see it. It is against this background that I would want to read the story of creation in *Genesis* (307 ff.) and let it make its own impact. Here is the same awe and the same wonder, and the primitiveness of its 'science' in no way diminishes its insight—which great scientists today (for whom the 'science' of *Genesis* is a mere relic of the past) can share. The kind of vision the Bible enshrines of the

[1] *The Listener*, 13.7.72, pp. 33f.

world and God and man can survive this kind of comparison, and even be really seen for what it is. [1]

Young people need to be helped, if they are to understand the Bible, to look at it against the background of what is happening in our own time. I would want to take the issues raised, for example, in a book like Geoffrey Barraclough's *An Introduction to Contemporary History*. I would read through the book and then ask 'What are some of the main issues our twentieth century raises, as this book sees them? How can I put them simply for young people to grasp and discuss?' And I would then want to look again with them at the issues the Bible itself raises as it looks its own world squarely in the face.

Roger W. Young's *Everybody's Business* is an excellent approach to the issues our present-day experience raises and as an approach to dealing with the insights and convictions of the Bible.

I would also want to introduce young people to men and women who in our own time have taken their part in its public life and for whom the Bible has mattered—people like William Temple, Dietrich Bonhoeffer, Dag Hammerskeld who cannot be charged with obscurantism or unawareness of our human predicament.

I hope that *Winding Quest* and *New World* will help the teacher in this give and take of classroom discussion. There is nothing to be afraid of; the Bible can look after itself—if it is seen to be the book it is. I have not tried to disguise the fact that it is a book from the ancient world—it is, as I have said, a particular story about a particular people; but I have tried, in both language and set-up, to make clear too that I think it is a universal story for everybody everywhere.

It is for young people themselves to make up their own minds. We should not underestimate their ability to tackle serious issues or to work out their own answers to the questions they raise, if these are presented to them in ways that are meaningful to them and in language that is untechnical and familiar. The greater demands that it makes upon the teacher are worth it.

Direct or indirect?

The answer is surely—both.

[1] A teacher should explore books like J.Z. Young's *An Introduction to the Study of Man* and A.R. Peacocke's *Science and the Christian Experiment* where man's place in the physical universe is faced.

When we are introducing young people to the Bible or want to stimulate their genuine interest and help them to see something of its meaning for today, we could profitably start with some issue the young people feel keenly about or which is dominating the public mind; then, when the discussion is reaching its important point to say 'Now this is just the point Amos—or Jeremiah or Jesus or Paul—was concerned with: listen to this' and quote briefly something they had to say that is to the point.

If some story or poem in an English lesson has caught their imagination, why shouldn't the teacher say to them 'I hear you were thrilled with such and such a story or poem. Here is a story—or poem—like it. Listen.'—and then read them a story or poem from the Bible which has the same dramatic or moving qualities.

Here is what John Austin Baker, a theologian, has to say about this indirect approach:

> To start from human life in the context of God and to see where, for us, the argument leads; and then to say, 'Look! in his own situation this was the kind of insight which Paul or John or Jesus was expressing'—this is of infinitely more value (than the more direct approach commonly used), because it brings home to the reader that the great perspective in which the Scriptures view human life is one that he can usefully adopt for himself. It gives him not a series of piecemeal dogmatic statements but a way of looking at existence, and a growing confidence that he can use it and get reliable results. As he does so, he then discovers for himself more and more in the Scriptures with which he has a feeling of kinship. Sometimes he will exclaim, as we all do in our ordinary reading, 'That is just what I wanted to say, but could never have put so well.' Then the scriptural language will become definitive for him. Sometimes he will prefer to put it in his own way, but will nevertheless develop a deepening respect for the Scriptures. Sometimes he will be led on to expand his own outlook by seeing that the biblical writers themselves move on from the point he shares with them; but he will do so by pondering for himself on life as he knows it, and only then discovering that they have been there before him. In this way he grows into the mind of the Bible, but he remains his own man and lives in his own day. Finally, and this is equally important, there will be times when he concludes that certain pronouncements of Scripture are mistaken or inadequate . . . What is vitally necessary is that people should not be encouraged to feel that in reaching such a decision on any particular point they are 'sinning' or inevitably mistaken. [1]

I have quoted this in full, not only for its wisdom, but for the teacher to be reassured that this approach is a theologically sound one;

[1] *The Foolishness of God*, p. 366 f.

in adopting it in the classroom, he is moving towards a proper adult attitude. The last sentences of the quotation are especially to be noted.

But all this is prolegomena to the proper dealing with the Bible. The time comes—and of this time the teacher himself must judge—when the Bible must be approached directly. I have said enough to show how enthralling much of it is. But it is the whole vision of the Bible that matters—it is much more than commentary on twentieth-century questions and problems—and it must be read and explored for its own sake. I have tried to make the arrangement of *Winding Quest* and *New World* such that the teacher can use them easily whether his approach to the biblical material is indirect or direct.

Themes

The indirect approach is really a theme approach, the themes coming from young people's own experience or from what is happening in our world today, questions they want to ask or events they feel deeply about.

But themes can arise from the Bible itself, and this is a very lively and proper approach. These themes can be of situation or of imagery.

Examples of themes of situation are: attitudes towards foreigners in stories from the first three parts of *Winding Quest*; in Amos's poetry; in the prophet of the Exile Servant Songs (289, 291, 295, 296); in *Ruth* (349) and *Jonah* (346) and *Daniel* (371 ff.); and then in *New World*: in the stories about Jesus and in his own stories; in Luke's writings (*NW* 142, 163, 311); in Paul (*NW* 287, 307 f., 323).

Situations in which we can see how men who tried to speak in God's name were received: Amos (233); Jeremiah (249, 253, 261); Jesus (*NW* 39–41); and Paul (*NW* 242, 246, 248). How men spoke of God's love and care: Prophet of the Exile (289); Ps. 91 (385); Ps. 104 (387); Ps. 121 (396); Ps. 139 (403); Ps. 23 (406); Jesus (*NW* 97 ff.); Paul (*NW* 307).

The world of nature is God's world: The story of creation (307); Ps. 29 (386); Ps. 104 (387); Ps. 148 (389); Jesus (*NW* 70, 82, 97, 104).

Themes of imagery are more difficult, for in dealing with imagery we must not treat it as though it existed apart from its setting. The teacher should note as he reads the way imagery is used. For example, he can take my sketch of Amos's world, p.60 and see how he has actually used the imagery in his poems; or note how Jesus uses the imagery Dr. Dodd has brought together on pp. 148 ff. in his *The Authority of the Bible*.

Examples of the enduring imagery of the Bible worth exploring are Light and Darkness (Day and Night); the Desert and the City; the Road or the Way. [1]

If we are not careful, we can easily use images in a mechanical or artificial way; we must remember that they are rooted in a poet's experience and cannot be divorced from it. Young people should be encouraged to look out for the imagery as they read and note the living way in which it is used. They could compare it with the use of imagery in modern poetry.

The best guide to this approach to the Bible is to note the way literature is dealt with by those professionally concerned with it in school. There has been an important revolution in the way poetry and prose are now approached, and we have much to learn from it in our dealing with the Bible.

On to the full translations

We come now to a most important matter. I have always described *New World* as 'first steps' to the New Testament. *Winding Quest* is, in the same way, 'first steps' to the Old Testament. They are both intended to help people who would never seriously open a full edition of the Bible and those who, if they did, would not know how to read it properly in a way that really helps them in their religious life. I think we have gravely misjudged the situation if we imagine that there are really many people who can open so large a book written so long ago and read it straight off as it lies before them with any profit or real understanding. And now we have the work of scholars to help us to understand it, a remarkable situation arises; they have made abundantly clear that the theme of the Bible is the simplicity of God's approach to us—his 'steadfast love' in the Old Testament and his 'love' in the New: this is given its supreme expression in Jesus's use of 'Abba' ('Father');

[1] For a discussion of the importance of the imagery of the 'Way' or 'Road' in Biblical thinking see E.J. Tinsley, *The Imitation of God in Christ*, pp. 31 ff., 67 ff. It was because of the associations of 'Way' in the Old Testament, I used it to translate 'The Kingdom of God'—'God's Way'. The first Christians callled themselves 'The People of the Way'.

yet at the same time they have shown us how complex in making and
form the Bible is. And we end up with serious Christians reading more
books about the Bible than reading the Bible itself. Their knowledge is
secondhand; this is clear in any discussions about the Bible in adult
groups. It will be already clear how I have planned *Winding Quest* and
New World to meet this situation—they are 'first steps' to the richness
of the Bible.

But first steps are only first steps; the teacher should, especially in
the higher forms in Secondary Schools, guide young people from the
'first steps' to some acquaintance with the full text in the splendid
translations now available. Here are some ways in which this could be
done.

1. I have tried in both *Winding Quest* and *New World* to give the
'heart' of the Bible as I have myself read it and learned from it. And
by this I do not mean only the heart of its historical story but also
the heart of its meaning. I have constantly emphasized the need to
encourage in young people 'critical awareness' and I think, at the
appropriate moment, that they could look critically at what I have
done—and feel free to disagree with me if they read the evidence
differently.

(a) I have simplified sometimes by following only one source when
the original story was a weaving of, perhaps, two sources and
editorial comment (see Appendix A). With a copy of the Revised
Standard Version of the Bible (which I judge best for this kind of
work) the teacher should take young people over what I have done:
for example, The Escape from Egypt (93 ff.); What Sort of Persons
should we be? (319).

(b) Sometimes, because of the need to reduce the length of a passage
or because of the complexity of the argument, I have had to paraphrase and this should be tested: for example, Baruch's rather prosy
style in his 'Story of Jeremiah' (247 ff.); but particularly in Paul's
letters (cf *NW* 301—the whole treatment of the great argument in
Romans 1–8 needs study) and the Fourth Gospel ('Table Talk',
NW 393 ff.).

(c) The poetry of the Bible has been added to, commented on and
rearranged by the editors for their own very good purposes. I have
given young people, as a first step, what scholars believe to be the

original form of the poetry of the prophets or of Jesus. I have therefore tried to give a critical arrangement of it. Young people should be encouraged to see what the setting of such poetry actually is and what I have done. This is especially necessary where, as with the stories and poetry of Jesus, we have two or even three versions and two or even three arrangements. I suggest the following poetry for examination: Amos—God's Way; the Common Law of the World (236); 'You did not come back to me' (240); 'The Confessions of Jeremiah' (262 ff.; here the teacher would do well to take young people through the argument of John Skinner's chapter XI in his study of Jeremiah, *Prophecy and Religion*); the parables of Jesus ('Girls at a Wedding', *NW* 67; 'A Royal Wedding', *NW* 91; 'Three Slaves', *NW* 84) and selected 'Sayings of Jesus' (*NW* 117 ff.) where he can see that the gospel writers either found these in collections of sayings and quoted the collection, attached them to what they judged to be appropriate parables or situations, or rearranged them, as in *Matthew* 5–7.

2. There is much other important material in the Bible I have selected which should be explored. Examples are: other and probably later sources which enrich the story; similar material which I did not use because I judged my selection sufficient; the full books from which I give only a few brief quotations, and books which I have not used at all (largely because of the pressure of space); the full argument, as in Paul's letters and the Fourth Gospel, where I have summarized and paraphrased.

3. The first steps of *Winding Quest* and *New World* are necessary if young people are to get a sense of the richness of the Bible. But now the wide story of the Bible lies before them in the full editions and they should be encouraged to explore both their contents and their pattern. I have included a chart in *Winding Quest* to show its relationship to the full Old Testament (as it appears in the Hebrew Bible).

4. I have reserved the Synoptic gospels for special comment. I was concerned in *New World* with helping the young reader to get a picture of the sort of person Jesus was as his friends remembered him, and I used *Mark* for this purpose. But I did not set out to give a proper edition of *Mark*. I gave also an edition of the parables and poetry of Jesus (again from his friends' memories of what he said) arranged

to help the reader to get something of the impact the sayings made
when first spoken. I was not, at this point, concerned with what any of
the evangelists thought they meant. I think that the way we often deal
with the sayings of Jesus is haphazard and superficial. I wanted young
people to feel something of the impact of his whole vision in his own
words. It is that vision that matters, not dry theological summaries of
his 'teaching'.

But this done, young people should go on to see something of the
vision of the men who first put down in some logical form, what his
friends remembered of Jesus, not as 'biographies' but as proclamations
of the Good News—what Jesus meant to men. So it is important that
young people should be encouraged to tackle the full gospels as books
to be read (not textbooks to be studied) and to be enjoyed.

In particular, I should add something about the Birth Stories, which
I did not include. I hope sometime to make a proper edition of these
to guide teachers. But here I would simply add that I left them out (I
originally planned to put them in) because without much more space
than I could afford, I could not do them justice. They come at the
end of the story when in Paul's letters and the Fourth Gospel the
heights have been reached; and they dramatize the great convictions
about Jesus which Paul and John set forth. 'The unique simplicity of
these narratives,' writes J.W. Bowman, 'together with their undoubted
wish to set the birth of Jesus in the framework of the Hebrew prophetic
teaching, suggests . . . that they represent the Church's attempt to
dramatize for popular understanding its faith in the genuine eternity
of the Son's Nature'. [1]

5. So the sweep of the whole Bible comes into view. Instead of being a
strange book full of 'obscure passages', it should now be seen as a book
worth living with. The principle on which I approach *Winding Quest*
and *New World* can now be applied to the whole Bible; it is there to
be enjoyed, explored and understood.

A FINAL WORD

I have one conviction in all my teaching of the Bible and it is this
conviction which lies at the back of both *Winding Quest* and *New
World*: that both young people and ordinary readers today do not need

[1] Peake's *Commentary on the Bible* (1962 edition), 639b.

to be 'spoon-fed'. The sooner they are 'exposed to the original sources' (as one historian puts it) the better, so that they can enter, as modern scholarship has made possible, into that conversation with men and women of the past which is part of true wisdom. This is true for the general history of humanity; it is especially true for the literature of the Bible.

I end with words I copied out when I first read them as a description of the kind of teacher of the Bible I ought to be. They were written by W.H. Auden as a summary of the function of a literary critic; but with the slight adjustment they require I take them for myself: [1]

So far as I am concerned he can do for me one or more of the following services:

1. Introduce me to authors or works of which I was hitherto unaware.

2. Convince me that I had undervalued an author or a work because I had not read them carefully enough.

3. Show me relations between works of different ages and cultures which I could never have seen for myself because I do not know enough and never shall.

4. Give a 'reading' of a work which increases my understanding of it.

5. Throw light upon the process of artistic 'making'.

6. Throw light upon the relation of art to life, to science, economics, ethics, religion.

And he adds:

The one thing I most emphatically do not ask of a critic is that he tell me what I *ought* to approve or condemn. I have no objection to his telling me what works or authors he likes and dislikes . . . But let him not dare to lay down the law to me. The responsibility for what I choose to read is mine, and nobody else on earth can do it for me. [1]

---

[1] *The Dyer's Hand*, p.8. For 'critic' read 'teacher'; for 'artistic "making" ' read 'the making of convictions'; for 'art' read 'the Bible'.

Appendix A

This note is to supplement what I have said about sources on pp.39 f. and 56 f.

I have used 'E' in 'Back to the highlands' (320–the latter part); 'Test of loyalty' (323); 'Brothers' quarrel' (325); 'Night at Bethel' (327); 'Escape south' (330); 'Boasting boy' (333); Brothers' revenge (333); 'Egyptian slave' (335 f.,– second half); 'Viceroy' (337); 'The last test' (345). In *Memories of the Past* I have occasionally supplemented the 'J' material with material from 'E'. 'The death of Moses' (from *Deuteronomy* and *Numbers*) is from 'E' (117).

'J' and 'E' were made into a single document sometime after the fall of Samaria in 721 B.C.E.; it is often not possible to separate the two traditions. I have used 'JE' in 'The desert march' (107); 'The ten words' (*Exodus* 18.20–25 – 109) and in 'The march to the river' (111 ff.).

I have used 'P' in 'The ten words) (*Exodus* 19.2–3, 7–8, 10–16; 20.2–17 – 117) and in 'The making of the Covenant' (110), as well as for the story of creation on pp. 307 f.

The Book of *Psalms* has a long history behind it. It consists of five books (an imitation of the five rolls of the Torah?): Book I – 1–41; Book II – 42–72; Book III – 73–89; Book IV – 90–106; Book V – 107–150. But behind the present first three books are two collections of hymns, one of which used 'Yahweh' for the name of God, the other 'Elohim'. The Yahwistic psalms are: 2–32; 34–41; 51–72. The Elohistic psalms are: 42–50; 73–83. It will be noted that the editors of the hymnbook included, for reasons we do not now know, a group of Yahwistic psalms with the Elohistic psalms of Book II. The last two books have no obvious divisions as have the first three.

The teacher would do well to make his own marked Bible where he can indicate, in a broad way, the sources from which the writings come. Whether these sources were oral or written is a disputed question; in later times they were certainly written sources, though stories were still being handed on by word of mouth. G.W. Anderson's *A Critical Introduction to the Old Testament* and the much fuller *The Old Testament: an Introduction* by Otto Eissfeldt will give him all the help he needs.

Appendix B

A real book about real people
Some suggested readings

Winding Quest

Shorter readings

Longer readings

New World

Shorter readings

SOME POETRY TO EXPLORE

Appendix C

The Sources of Mark
(From V. Taylor: *The Gospel according to St. Mark*, esp. 78 ff.)

Source	Mark	New World
Early Witnesses		
Baptism and Temptation	1.2–13	3–5
The Leper	1.40–44	13
Storm on the Lake	4.35–41	13
The Gerasene Madman	5.1–20	14
Jairus's Daughter	5.21–24, 35–43	17
The Sick Woman	5.25–34	17
The Desert Meal	6.35–44	25
Walking on the Water	6.45–52	26
The Foreign Woman	7.25–30	27
The Deaf-mute	7.32–37	18
No Sign!	8.11–13	–
A Blind Man	8.22–26	18
The Epileptic Boy	9.14–29	30
The Jericho Beggar	10.47–52	35
The Fig Tree	11.13 f., 20–22	–
Eyewitness's Memories (Peter?)		
A Day in the Life of Jesus	1.16–39	(10) 6
The Sick of the Palsy	2.3–5, 11 f.	14
The Call of Levi	2.14	10
The Comments of Nazareth	6.3–6	9
The Highland Road	8.27–33	28
The Mountain Climb	9.3–8	29
The Rich Young Man	10.17–22	10
What shall we get?	10.23–30	10
James and John	10.35–40	35
The Ride into the City	11.1b–10	37
The Temple Incident	11.16–18	39
Memories of the Last Days:		
Bethany	14.3–9	45
The Bread and the Cup	14.22–25	47
The Orchard	14.32–42	49
The High Priest's Officer	14.47–52	49
Peter's Denial	14.54, 66–72	51
Before Pilate	15.2, 6–14	52
The Soldiers	15.16–20	53
The Death and Burial of Jesus	15, 25, 27, 31–33, 38, 40 f., 47	53 f.

Source	*Mark*	*New World*
Popular Stories		
Pharisaic Critics	2.6–10; 15–17; 10.1–9	–; 20; –;
	11.27–33; 12.13–17	39; 41
John's Disciples	2.18–20	21
The Sabbath Day	2.23–26	21
The Withered Hand	3.1–5	22
He hath Beelzebub	3.22–26	–
Jesus's Family	3.31–35	9
John's Murder	6.17–29	–
The Pharisees	7.1–13	22
John Rebuked	9.38 f.	34
Little Children	10.13–16	20
Sadducean Critics	12.18–27	–
The First Commandment	12.28–34	42
David's Son	12.35–37	–
The Widow's Mite	12.41–44	43
The Temple Ruins	13.1 f.	66

The 'Lesson Book' of the Church in Italy

2.21 f.; 2.27 f.; 3.27–30; 4.2b–9; 4.13–32; 7.14–23; 8.34–9.1; 9.37; 40–50; 10.11 f.; 31; 11.23–25; 12.1–12; 38–40; 13.6–8, 24–27; 9–13; 19–23; 28 f.; 30; 31; 32; 33; 34; 35–37. (See Index).

The Passion Story of the Church in Italy

14. 1 f, 10 f, 17–21, 43–46, 53, 55–64; *15.* 1, 3–5, 15, 21–24, 26, 29 f, 34–37, 39, 42–46; (*16.* 1–8?)

In *New World* the Passion Story will be found under the title 'The Great Feast' at pp.45 ff. (omitting 'In Bethany', 'Finding the House', 'In the Street' and 'The Soldiers', and adjusting the others).

Appendix D

Jesus and his People's Story
Suggested readings

Winding Quest

The Exodus from Egypt

'Not our fathers' swords . . . but the light of
your presence'   Ps. 44.3 (398)

The Story in Song

Dance, O Earth!   Psalm 114 (205)
Tell the whole world!   Psalm 105 (203)

The Story in Law

Harvest Declaration   Deut. 26.1–2, 5–11
                                                  (189)

Generosity for everybody   Deut. 24.6, 10–22 (188)

A Story for the World as we know it?

'How deep is the human heart—deep as an
    unfathomable sea!
Its sickness defies cure—who knows it secret?'—Jeremiah 17.9–10 (264)

Every man for himself?

The March to the North   Judges 17–18 (135)
Brothers' Quarrel   Genesis 27.1–45 (325)

And at the mercy of the big battalions?

The Death of a City
    In the besieged City   Jer, 37.1–21; 38.1–28
                                                  (253)

Freedom again   Jer. 39.1–3, 13–18;
                                                  40.1–6 (256)

Murder of the Governor   Jer. 7–16; 41.1–18 (257)

Varied Response

'How can we sing God's song—anywhere?'   Ps. 137.4 (214)
National Lament   Psalm 74 (209)
Bitter Anger   Psalm 137 (214)
There's nothing worth living for!   Eccles. 1.2–11; 2.12–17
                                                  (379)

But God still means everything to me   Psalm 23 (386)

A Prophet's Insight

'There's to be a new Exodus—prepare God's way
through the desert'   Isa. 40.3 (285)

The Road Home	Isaiah 40
Our slavery is over!	verses 1–2 (285)
The Voice	3–8 (285)
Good News!	9–11 (286)
A word to the world	12–18, 21–26 (287)
A word to God's people	27–31 (289)
Four songs: God's Servant–a Man for others	
First Song	Isaiah 42.1–4 (289)
Second Song	Isaiah 49.1–6 (291)
Third Song	Isaiah 50.4–9 (295)
Fourth Song*	Isaiah 52.13–53.12 (296)
	New World

The Servant

'I came to be a servant'	Mark 10.45 (35)
Jesus–Servant	John 13.1–17 (393)
Table Talk	John 13.21–16.33
	(393 ff.)
Prayer in the Upper Room	John 17 (398)

* This poem has got disarranged in being handed down. This may have been the original order: 52.13, 14a, 15; 53.1–2; 52.14b; 53.3–12.

Note: the death of Jesus took place at the time of the celebration by his people of the Exodus from Egypt–the Passover Meal.

Appendix E

The Difference Jesus has made
Some suggested readings from New World

NOTE: We begin with the story of the death of Jesus because it was this event
that brought home to his friends the reality of God's love and stung them into
thought and action. We then move on to stories about him that his friends remembered and a personal account of the difference Jesus had made to one man—Paul.
Then come statements by three friends. For background the teacher should read
Dr. C.H. Dodd's *The Founder of Christianity* and T.W. Manson's *The Servant-
Messiah.*

FOR FURTHER READING

(to supplement books already mentioned in the text or in
Winding Quest and *New World*

The best book on the making of the Bible, set against the history out of which it rose, is Jan H. Negeman, *New Atlas of the Bible* (Collins); for the New Testament itself see C.F.D. Moule, *The Birth of the New Testament* (A. and C. Black) which shows how the New Testament rose out of the life and experience of the early Christian community.

For the historical background of the Old Testament, see either N.K. Gottwald, *A Light to the Nations* (Harper and Row) or J. Bright, *A History of Israel* (S.C.M.); and D. Winton Davies, *Documents from Old Testament Times* (Nelson).

For the historical background of the New Testament, see Floyd V. Filson, *A New Testament History* (S.C.M.); C.K. Barrett, *The New Testament Background: Selected Documents* (S.P.C.K.); Y. Yadin, *Masada* (Weidenfeld and Nicolson)— magnificently illustrating the Resistance Movement.

On Old Testament convictions, see H.H. Rowley's survey, *The Faith of Israel* (S.C.M.). On the prophets, see E.W. Heaton, *The Old Testament Prophets* (Pelican); N.K. Gottwald, *All the Kingdoms of the Earth* (Harper and Row) is a stimulating account of the prophets in the world of their time. On the Psalms, see Helmer Ringgren, *The Faith of the Psalmists* (S.C.M.).

On Jesus see T.W. Manson, *The Servant-Messiah* (C.U.P.); C.H. Dodd, *The Founder of Christianity* (Collins); G. Bornkamm, *Jesus of Nazareth* (Hodder and Stoughton); T.W. Manson, *The Teaching of Jesus*; J. Jeremias, *The Parables of Jesus* (S.C.M.).

For classroom work on the background of Jesus's ministry and the Resistance Movement, see Brian Brown, *The Choice* and *The Search* (Denholme House Press).

On Paul see A.M. Hunter, *Paul and his Predecessors* (Nicholson and Watson); John Knox, *Chapters in a Life of Paul* (A. and C. Black); G. Bornkamm, *Paul* (Hodder and Stoughton).

On the Fourth Gospel, see C.H. Dodd, *The Interpretation of the Fourth Gospel* and *Historical Tradition in the Fourth Gospel* (both C.U.P.).

On worship see A.S. Herbert, *Worship in Ancient Israel*; C.F.D. Moule, *Worship in the New Testament* (both Lutterworth Press).

For quick reference the teacher will find H.H. Rowley's three books most useful—*Dictionary of Bible Place Names*, *Dictionary of Bible Personal Names*, *Dictionary of Bible Themes* (all Nelson).

For a good general survey of biblical material see R.C. Walton (Editor) *A Source Book of the Bible for Teachers* (S.C.M.).

For an excellent discussion of the place of the Bible in religious education see Douglas S. Hubery, *Teaching the Christian Faith Today* (Chester House publication) and *Christian Education and the Bible* (National Christian Education Council).

For a biblical atlas, see *The Oxford Bible Atlas* (O.U.P.).